MEMOIRS OF MY
LIFE AND WRITINGS

In the fifty-second year of my age, after the completion of an arduous and successful work, I now propose to employ some moments of my leisure in reviewing the simple transactions of a private and literary life. Truth, naked unblushing truth, the first virtue of more serious history, must be the sole recommendation of this personal narrative. The style shall be simple and familiar; but style is the image of character; and the habits of correct writing may produce, without labour or design, the appearance of art and study. My own amusement is my motive, and will be my reward: and if these sheets are communicated to some discreet and indulgent friends, they will be secreted from the public eye till the author shall be removed beyond the reach of criticism or ridicule.

A lively desire of knowing and of recording our ancestors so generally prevails, that it must depend on the influence of some common principle in the minds of men. We seem to have lived in the persons of our forefathers; it is the labour and reward of vanity to extend the term of this ideal longevity. Our imagination is always active to enlarge the narrow circle in which Nature has confined us. Fifty or an hundred years may be allotted to an individual, but we step forward beyond death with such hopes as religion and philosophy will suggest; and we fill up the silent vacancy that precedes our birth, by associating ourselves to the authors of our existence. Our calmer judgment will rather tend to moderate, than to suppress, the pride of an ancient and worthy race. The satirist may laugh, the philosopher may preach; but Reason herself will respect the prejudices and habits, which have been consecrated by the experience of mankind.

Wherever the distinction of birth is allowed to form a superior order in the state, education and example should always, and will often, produce among them a dignity of sentiment and propriety of conduct, which is guarded from dishonour by their own and the public esteem. If we read of some illustrious line so ancient that it has no beginning, so worthy that it ought to have no end, we sympathize in its various fortunes; nor can we blame the generous enthusiasm, or even the harmless vanity, of those who are allied to the honours of its name. For my own part, could I draw my pedigree from a general, a statesman, or a celebrated author, I should study their lives with the diligence of filial love. In the investigation of past events, our curiosity is stimulated by the immediate or indirect reference to ourselves; but in the estimate of honour we should learn to value the gifts of Nature above those of Fortune; to esteem in our ancestors the qualities that best promote the interests of society; and to pronounce the descendant of a king less truly noble than the offspring of a man of genius, whose writings will instruct or delight the latest posterity. The family of Confucius is, in my opinion, the most illustrious in the world. After a painful ascent of eight or ten centuries, our barons and princes of Europe are lost in the darkness of the middle ages; but, in the vast equality of the empire of China, the posterity of Confucius have maintained, above two thousand two hundred years, their peaceful honours and perpetual succession. The chief of the family is still revered, by the sovereign and the people, as the lively image of the wisest of mankind. The nobility of the Spencers has been illustrated and enriched by the trophies of Marlborough; but I exhort them to consider the "Fairy Queen" as the most precious jewel of their coronet. I have exposed my private feelings, as I shall always do, without scruple or reserve. That these sentiments are just, or at least natural, I am inclined to believe, since I do not feel myself interested in the cause; for I can derive from my ancestors neither glory nor shame.

Yet a sincere and simple narrative of my own life may amuse some of my leisure hours; but it will subject me, and perhaps with justice, to the imputation of vanity. I may judge, however, from the experience both of past and of the present times, that the public are always curious to know the men, who have left behind them any image of their minds: the most scanty accounts of such men are compiled with diligence, and perused with eagerness; and the student of every class may derive a lesson, or an example, from the lives most similar to his own. My name may hereafter be placed among the thousand articles of a Biographic Britannica; and I must be conscious, that no one is so well qualified, as myself, to describe the series of my thoughts and actions. The authority of my masters, of the grave Thuanus, and the philosophic Hume, might be sufficient to justify my design; but it would not be difficult to produce a long list of ancients and moderns, who, in various forms, have exhibited their own portraits. Such portraits are often the most interesting, and sometimes the only interesting parts of their writings; and if they be sincere, we seldom complain of the minuteness or prolixity of these personal memorials. The lives of the younger Pliny, of Petrarch, and of Erasmus, are expressed in the epistles, which they themselves have given to the world. The essays of Montaigne and Sir William Temple bring us home to the houses and bosoms of the authors: we smile without contempt at the headstrong passions of Benevenuto Cellini, and the gay follies of Colley Cibber. The confessions of St. Austin and Rousseau disclose the secrets of the human heart; the commentaries of the learned Huet have survived his evangelical demonstration; and the memoirs of Goldoni are more truly dramatic than his Italian comedies. The heretic and the churchman are strongly marked in the characters and fortunes of Whiston and Bishop Newton; and even the dullness of Michael de Marolles and Anthony Wood acquires some value from the faithful representation of men and manners. That I am equal or superior to some of these, the effects of modesty or affectation cannot force me to dissemble.

My family is originally derived from the county of Kent. The Southern district, which borders on Sussex and the sea, was formerly overspread with the great forest Anderida, and even now retains the denomination of the Weald or Woodland. In this district, and in the hundred and parish of Rolvenden, the Gibbons were possessed of lands in the year one thousand three hundred and twenty-six; and the elder branch of the family, without much increase or diminution of property, still adheres to its native soil. Fourteen years after the first appearance of his name, John Gibbon is recorded as the Marmorarius or architect of King Edward the Third: the strong and stately castle of Queensborough, which guarded the entrance of the Medway, was a monument of his skill; and the grant of an hereditary toll on the passage from Sandwich to Stonar, in the Isle of Thanet, is the reward of no vulgar artist. In the visitations of the heralds, the Gibbons are frequently mentioned; they held the rank of esquire in an age, when that title was less promiscuously assumed: one of them, under the reign of Queen Elizabeth, was captain of the militia of Kent; and a free school, in the neighbouring town of Benenden, proclaims the charity and opulence of its founder. But time, or their own obscurity, has cast a veil of oblivion over the virtues and vices of my Kentish ancestors; their character or station confined them to the labours and pleasures of a rural life: nor is it in my power to follow the advice of the poet, in an inquiry after a name,—

"Go! search it there, where to be born, and die,

Of rich and poor makes all the history." So recent is the institution of our parish registers. In the beginning of the seventeenth century, a younger branch of the Gibbons of Rolvenden migrated from the country to the city; and from this branch I do not blush to descend. The law requires some abilities; the church imposes some restraints; and before our army and navy, our civil establishments, and India empire, had opened so many paths of fortune, the mercantile profession was more frequently chosen by youths of a liberal race and education, who aspired to create their own independence. Our most respectable families have not disdained the counting-house, or even the shop; their names are enrolled in the Livery and Companies of London; and in England, as well as in the Italian commonwealths, heralds have been compelled to declare that gentility is not degraded by the exercise of trade.

The armorial ensigns which, in the times of chivalry, adorned the crest and shield of the soldier, are now become an empty decoration, which every man, who has money to build a carriage, may paint according to his fancy on the panels. My family arms are the same, which were borne by the Gibbons of Kent in an age, when the College of Heralds religiously guarded the distinctions of blood and name: a lion rampant gardant, between three schallop-shells argent, on a field azure. I should not however have been tempted to blazon my coat of arms, were it not connected with a whimsical anecdote. About the reign of James the First, the three harmless schallop-shells were changed by Edmund Gibbon esq. into three ogresses, or female cannibals, with a design of stigmatizing three ladies, his kinswomen, who had provoked him by an unjust law-suit. But this singular mode of revenge, for which he obtained the sanction of Sir William Seagar, king at arms, soon expired with its author; and, on his own monument in the Temple church, the monsters vanish, and the three schallop-shells resume their proper and hereditary place.

Our alliances by marriage it is not disgraceful to mention. The chief honour of my ancestry is James Fiens, Baron Say and Scale, and Lord High Treasurer of England, in the reign of Henry the Sixth; from whom by the Phelips, the Whetnalls, and the Cromers, I am lineally descended in the eleventh degree. His dismission and imprisonment in the Tower were insufficient to appease the popular clamour; and the Treasurer, with his son-in-law Cromer, was beheaded(1450), after a mock trial by the Kentish insurgents. The black list of his offences, as it is exhibited in Shakespeare, displays the ignorance and envy of a plebeian tyrant. Besides the vague reproaches of selling Maine and Normandy to the Dauphin, the Treasurer is specially accused of luxury, for riding on a foot-cloth; and of treason, for speaking French, the language of our enemies: "Thou hast most traitorously corrupted the youth of the realm," says Jack Cade to the unfortunate Lord, "in erecting a grammar-school; and whereas before our forefathers had no other books than the score and the tally, thou hast caused printing to be used; and, contrary to the king, his crown, and dignity, thou hast built a paper-mill. It will be proved to thy face, that thou hast men about thee, who usually talk of a noun and a verb, and such abominable words, as no Christian ear can endure to hear." Our dramatic poet is generally more attentive to character than to history; and I much fear that the art of printing was not introduced into England, till several years after Lord Say's death; but of some of these meritorious crimes I should hope to find my ancestor guilty; and a man of letters may be proud of his descent from a patron and martyr of learning.

In the beginning of the last century Robert Gibbon Esq. of Rolvenden in Kent (who died in 1618), had a son of the same name of Robert, who settled in London, and became a member of the Cloth-workers' Company. His wife was a daughter of the Edgars, who flourished about four hundred years in the county of Suffolk, and produced an eminent and wealthy serjeant-at-law, Sir Gregory Edgar, in the reign of Henry the Seventh. Of the sons of Robert Gibbon, (who died in 1643,) Matthew did not aspire above the station of a linen-draper in Leadenhall-street; but John has given to the public some curious memorials of his existence, his character, and his family. He was born on Nov. 3d, 1629; his education was liberal, at a grammar- school, and afterwards in Jesus College at Cambridge; and he celebrates the retired content which he enjoyed at Allesborough, in Worcestershire, in the house of Thomas Lord Coventry, where John Gibbon was employed as a domestic tutor, the same office which Mr. Hobbes exercised in the Devonshire family. But the spirit of my kinsman soon immerged into more active life: he visited foreign countries as a soldier and a traveller, acquired the knowledge of the French and Spanish languages, passed some time in the Isle of Jersey, crossed the Atlantic, and resided upwards of a twelvemonth (1659) in the rising colony of Virginia. In this remote province his taste, or rather passion, for heraldry found a singular gratification at a war-dance of the native Indians. As they moved in measured steps, brandishing their tomahawks, his curious eye contemplated their little shields of bark, and their naked bodies, which were painted with the colours and symbols of his favourite science. "At which I exceedingly wondered; and concluded that heraldry was ingrafted *naturally* into the sense of human race. If so, it deserves a greater esteem than now-a-days is put upon it." His return to England after the Restoration was soon followed by his marriage his settlement in a house in St. Catherine's Cloister, near the Tower, which devolved to my grandfather and his introduction into the Heralds' College (in 1671) by the style and title of Blue-mantle Pursuivant at Arms. In this office he enjoyed near fifty years the rare felicity of uniting, in the same pursuit, his duty and inclination: his name is remembered in the College, and many of his letters are still preserved. Several of the most respectable characters of the age, Sir William Dugdale, Mr. Ashmole, Dr. John Betts, and Dr. Nehemiah Grew, were his friends; and in the society of such men, John Gibbon may be recorded without disgrace as the member of an astrological club. The study of hereditary honours is favourable to the Royal prerogative; and my kinsman, like most of his family, was a high Tory both in church and state. In the latter end of the reign of Charles the Second, his pen was exercised in the cause of the Duke of York: the Republican faction he most cordially detested; and as each animal is conscious of its proper arms, the heralds' revenge was emblazoned on a most diabolical escutcheon.

But the triumph of the Whig government checked the preferment of Blue-mantle; and he was even suspended from his office, till his tongue could learn to pronounce the oath of abjuration. His life was prolonged to the age of ninety: and, in the expectation of the inevitable though uncertain hour, he wishes to preserve the blessings of health, competence, and virtue. In the year 1682 he published in London his Introductio ad Latinam Blasoniam, an original attempt, which Camden had desiderated, to define, in a Roman idiom, the terms and attributes of a Gothic institution. It is not two years since I acquired, in a foreign land, some domestic intelligence of my own family; and this intelligence was conveyed to Switzerland from the heart of Germany. I had formed an acquaintance with Mr. Langer, a lively and ingenious scholar, while he resided at Lausanne as preceptor to the Hereditary Prince of Brunswick. On his return to his proper station of Librarian to the Ducal Library of Wolfenbuttel, he accidentally found among some literary rubbish a small old English volume of heraldry, inscribed with the name of John Gibbon. From the title only Mr. Langer judged that it might be an acceptable present to his friend—and he judged rightly. His manner is quaint and affected; his order is confused: but he displays some wit, more reading, and still more enthusiasm: and if an enthusiast be often absurd, he is never languid. An English text is perpetually interspersed with Latin sentences in prose and verse; but in his own poetry he claims an exemption from the laws of prosody. Amidst a profusion of genealogical knowledge, my kinsman could not be forgetful of his own name; and to him I am indebted for almost the whole of my information concerning the Gibbon family. From this small work the author expected immortal fame.

Such are the hopes of authors! In the failure of those hopes John Gibbon has not been the first of his profession, and very possibly may not be the last of his name. His brother Matthew Gibbon, the draper, had one daughter and two sons—my grandfather Edward, who was born in the year 1666, and Thomas, afterwards Dean of Carlisle. According to the mercantile creed, that the best book is a profitable ledger, the writings of John the herald would be much less precious than those of his nephew Edward: but an author professes at least to write for the public benefit; and the slow balance of trade can be pleasing to those persons only, to whom it is advantageous. The successful industry of my grandfather raised him above the level of his immediate ancestors; he appears to have launched into various and extensive dealings: even his opinions were subordinate to his interest; and I find him in Flanders clothing King William's troops, while he would have contracted with more pleasure, though not perhaps at a cheaper rate, for the service of King James. During his residence abroad, his concerns at home were managed by his mother Hester, an active and notable woman. Her second husband was a widower of the name of Acton: they united the children of their first nuptials. After his marriage with the daughter of Richard Acton, goldsmith in Leadenhall-street, he gave his own sister to Sir Whitmore Acton, of Aldenham; and I am thus connected, by a triple alliance, with that ancient and loyal family of Shropshire baronets. It consisted about that time of seven brothers, all of gigantic stature; one of whom, a pigmy of six feet two inches, confessed himself the last and least of the seven; adding, in the true spirit of party, that such men were not born since the Revolution. Under the Tory administration of the four last years of Queen Anne (1710-1714) Mr. Edward Gibbon was appointed one of the Commissioners of the Customs; he sat at that Board with Prior; but the merchant was better qualified for his station than the poet; since Lord Bolingbroke has been heard to declare, that he had never conversed with a man, who more clearly understood the commerce and finances of England. In the year 1716 he was elected one of the Directors of the South Sea Company; and his books exhibited the proof that, before his acceptance of this fatal office, he had acquired an independent fortune of sixty thousand pounds.

But his fortune was overwhelmed in the shipwreck of the year twenty, and the labours of thirty years were blasted in a single day. Of the use or abuse of the South Sea scheme, of the guilt or innocence of my grandfather and his brother Directors, I am neither a competent nor a disinterested judge. Yet the equity of modern times must condemn the violent and arbitrary proceedings, which would have disgraced the cause of justice, and would render injustice still more odious. No sooner had the nation awakened from its golden dream, than a popular and even a parliamentary clamour demanded their victims: but it was acknowledged on all sides that the South Sea Directors, however guilty, could not be touched by any known laws of the land. The speech of Lord Molesworth, the author of the State of Denmark, may shew the temper, or rather the intemperance, of the House of Commons. "Extraordinary crimes (exclaimed that ardent Whig) call aloud for extraordinary remedies. The Roman lawgivers had not foreseen the possible existence of a parricide; but as soon as the first monster appeared, he was sewn in a sack, and cast headlong into the river; and I shall be content to inflict the same treatment on the authors of our present ruin." His motion was not literally adopted; but a bill of pains and penalties was introduced, a retroactive statute, to punish the offences, which did not exist at the time they were committed. Such a pernicious violation of liberty and law can be excused only by the most imperious necessity; nor could it be defended on this occasion by the plea of impending danger or useful example. The legislature restrained the persons of the Directors, imposed an exorbitant security for their appearance, and marked their characters with a previous note of ignominy: they were compelled to deliver, upon oath, the strict value of their estates; and were disabled from making any transfer or alienation of any part of their property. Against a bill of pains and penalties it is the common right of every subject to be heard by his counsel at the bar: they prayed to be heard; their prayer was refused; and their oppressors, who required no evidence, would listen to no defence. It had been at first proposed that one-eighth of their respective estates should be allowed for the future support of the Directors; but it was speciously urged, that in the various shades of opulence and guilt such an unequal proportion would be too light for many, and for some might possibly be too heavy. The character and conduct of each man were separately weighed; but, instead of the calm solemnity of a judicial inquiry, the fortune and honour of three and thirty Englishmen were made the topic of hasty conversation, the sport of a lawless majority; and the basest member of the committee, by a malicious word or, a silent vote, might indulge his general spleen or personal animosity. Injury was aggravated by insult, and insult was embittered by pleasantry. Allowances of twenty pounds, or one shilling, were facetiously moved. A vague report that a Director had formerly been concerned in another project, by which some unknown persons had lost their money, was admitted as a proof of his actual guilt. One man was ruined because he had dropped a foolish speech, that his horses should feed upon gold; another because he was grown so proud, that, one day at the Treasury, he had refused a civil answer to persons much above him. All were condemned, absent and unheard, in arbitrary fines and forfeitures, which swept away the greatest part of their substance. Such bold oppression can scarcely be shielded by the omnipotence of parliament; and yet it maybe seriously questioned, whether the judges of the South Sea Directors were the true and legal representatives of their country. The first parliament of George the First had been chosen (1715) for three years: the term had elapsed, their trust was expired; and the four additional years (1718-1722), during which they continued to sit, were derived not from the people, but from themselves; from the strong measure of the septennial bill, which can only be paralleled by il serar di consiglio of the Venetian history. Yet candour will own that to the same parliament every Englishman is deeply indebted: the septennial act, so vicious in its origin, has been sanctioned by time, experience, and the national consent. Its first operation secured the House of Hanover on the throne, and its permanent influence maintains the peace and stability of government. As often as a repeal has been moved in the House of Commons, I have given in its defence a clear and conscientious vote. My grandfather could not expect to be treated with more lenity than his companions. His Tory principles and connections rendered him obnoxious to the ruling powers: his name is reported in a suspicious secret; and his well-known abilities could not plead the excuse of ignorance or error. In the first proceedings against the South Sea Directors, Mr. Gibbon is one of the few who were taken into custody; and, in the final sentence, the measure of his fine proclaims him eminently guilty. The total estimate which he delivered on oath to the House of Commons amounted to 106,543 pounds 5 shillings and 6 pence, exclusive of antecedent settlements. Two different allowances of 15,000 pounds and of 10,000 pounds were moved for Mr. Gibbon; but, on the question being put, it was carried without a division for the smaller sum. On these ruins, with the skill and credit, of which parliament had not been able to despoil him, my grandfather at a mature age erected the edifice of a new fortune: the labours of sixteen years were amply rewarded; and I have reason to believe that the second structure was not much inferior to the first. He had realized a very considerable property in Sussex, Hampshire, Buckinghamshire, and the New River Company; and had acquired a spacious house, with gardens and lands, at Putney, in Surrey, where he resided in decent hospitality. He died in December 1736, at the age of seventy; and by his last will, at the expense of Edward, his only son, (with whose marriage he was not perfectly reconciled,) enriched his two daughters, Catherine and Hester. The former became the wife of Mr. Edward Elliston, an East India captain: their daughter and heiress Catherine was married in the year 1756 to Edward Eliot, Esq. (now lord Eliot), of Port Eliot, in the county of Cornwall; and their three sons are my nearest male relations on the father's side. A life of devotion and celibacy was the choice of my aunt, Mrs. Hester Gibbon, who, at the age of eighty-five, still resides in a hermitage at Cliffe, in Northamptonshire; having long survived her spiritual guide and faithful companion Mr. William Law, who, at an advanced age, about the year 1761, died in her house. In our family he had left the reputation of a worthy and pious man, who believed all that he professed, and practised all that he enjoined. The character of a non-juror, which he maintained to the last, is a sufficient evidence of his principles in church and state; and the sacrifice of interest to conscience will be always respectable. His theological writings, which our domestic connection has tempted me to peruse, preserve an imperfect sort of life, and I can pronounce with more confidence and knowledge on the merits of the author. His last compositions are darkly tinctured by the incomprehensible visions of Jacob Behmen; and his discourse on the absolute unlawfulness of stage entertainments is sometimes quoted for a ridiculous intemperance of sentiment and language.— "The actors and spectators must all be damned: the playhouse is the porch of Hell, the place of the Devil's abode, where he holds his filthy court of evil spirits: a play is the Devil's triumph, a sacrifice performed to his glory, as much as in the heathen temples of Bacchus or Venus, &c., &c." But these sallies of religious frenzy must not extinguish the praise, which is due to Mr. William Law as a wit and a scholar. His argument on topics of less absurdity is specious and acute, his manner is lively, his style forcible and clear; and, had not his vigorous mind been clouded by enthusiasm, he might be ranked with the most agreeable and ingenious writers of the times. While the Bangorian controversy was a fashionable theme, he entered the lists on the subject of Christ's kingdom, and the authority of the priesthood: against the plain account of the sacrament of the Lord's Supper he resumed the combat with Bishop Hoadley, the object of Whig idolatry, and Tory abhorrence; and at every weapon of attack and defence the non-juror, on the ground which is common to both, approves himself at least equal to the prelate. On the appearance of the Fable of the Bees, he drew his pen against the licentious doctrine that private vices are public benefits, and morality as well as religion must join in his applause. Mr. Law's master-work, the Serious Call, is still read as a popular and powerful book of devotion. His precepts are rigid, but they are founded on the gospel; his satire is sharp, but it is drawn from the knowledge of human life; and many of his portraits are not unworthy of the pen of La Bruyere. If he finds a spark of piety in his reader's mind, he will soon kindle it to a flame; and a philosopher must allow that he exposes, with equal severity and truth, the strange contradiction between the faith and practice of the Christian world. Under the names of Flavia and Miranda he has admirably described my two aunts the heathen and the Christian sister.

My father, Edward Gibbon, was born in October, 1707: at the age of thirteen he could scarcely feel that he was disinherited by act of parliament; and, as he advanced towards manhood, new prospects of fortune opened to his view. A parent is most attentive to supply in his children the deficiencies, of which he is conscious in himself: my grandfather's knowledge was derived from a strong understanding, and the experience of the ways of men; but my father enjoyed the benefits of a liberal education as a scholar and a gentleman. At Westminster School, and afterwards at Emanuel College in Cambridge, he passed through a regular course of academical discipline; and the care of his learning and morals was intrusted to his private tutor, the same Mr. William Law. But the mind of a saint is above or below the present world; and while the pupil proceeded on his travels, the tutor remained at Putney, the much-honoured friend and spiritual director of the whole family. My father resided sometime at Paris to acquire the fashionable exercises; and as his temper was warm and social, he indulged in those pleasures, for which the strictness of his former education had given him a keener relish. He afterwards visited several provinces of France; but his excursions were neither long nor remote; and the slender knowledge, which he had gained of the French language, was gradually obliterated. His passage through Besancon is marked by a singular consequence in the chain of human events. In a dangerous illness Mr. Gibbon was attended, at his own request, by one of his kinsmen of the name of Acton, the younger brother of a younger brother, who had applied himself to the study of physic. During the slow recovery of his patient, the physician himself was attacked by the malady of love: he married his mistress, renounced his country and religion, settled at Besancon, and became the father of three sons; the eldest of whom, General Acton, is conspicuous in Europe as the principal Minister of the king of the Two Sicilies. By an uncle whom another stroke of fortune had transplanted to Leghorn, he was educated in the naval service of the Emperor; and his valour and conduct in the command of the Tuscan frigates protected the retreat of the Spaniards from Algiers. On my father's return to England he was chosen, in the general election of 1734, to serve in parliament for the borough of Petersfield; a burgage tenure, of which my grandfather possessed a weighty share, till he alienated (I know not why) such important property. In the opposition to Sir Robert Walpole and the Pelhams, prejudice and society connected his son with the Tories,—shall I say Jacobites? or, as they were pleased to style themselves, the country gentlemen? with them he gave many a vote; with them he drank many a bottle. Without acquiring the fame of an orator or a statesman, he eagerly joined in the great opposition, which, after a seven years' chase, hunted down Sir Robert Walpole: and in the pursuit of an unpopular minister, he gratified a private revenge against the oppressor of his family in the South Sea persecution.

I was born at Putney, in the county of Surrey, April 27th, O. S., in the year one thousand seven hundred and thirty-seven; the first child of the marriage of Edward Gibbon, esq., and of Judith Porten. [Note: The union to which I owe my birth was a marriage of inclination and esteem. Mr. James Porten, a merchant of London, resided with his family at Putney, in a house adjoining to the bridge and churchyard, where I have passed many happy hours of my childhood. He left one son (the late Sir Stanier Porten) and three daughters; Catherine, who preserved her maiden name, and of whom I shall hereafter speak; another daughter married Mr. Darrel of Richmond, and left two sons, Edward and Robert:

the youngest of the three sisters was Judith, my mother.] My lot might have been that of a slave, a savage, or a peasant; nor can I reflect without pleasure on the bounty of Nature, which cast my birth in a free and civilized country, in an age of science and philosophy, in a family of honourable rank, and decently endowed with the gifts of fortune. From my birth I have enjoyed the right of primogeniture; but I was succeeded by five brothers and one sister, all of whom were snatched away in their infancy. My five brothers, whose names may be found in the parish register of Putney, I shall not pretend to lament: but from my childhood to the present hour I have deeply and sincerely regretted my sister, whose life was somewhat prolonged, and whom I remember to have been an amiable infant. The relation of a brother and a sister, especially if they do not marry, appears to me of a very singular nature. It is a familiar and tender friendship with a female, much about our own age; an affection perhaps softened by the secret influence of sex, and the sole species of Platonic love that can be indulged with truth, and without danger.

At the general election of 1741, Mr. Gibbon and Mr. Delme stood an expensive and successful contest at Southampton, against Mr. Dummer and Mr. Henly, afterwards Lord Chancellor and Earl of Northington. The Whig candidates had a majority of the resident voters; but the corporation was firm in the Tory interest: a sudden creation of one hundred and seventy new freemen turned the scale; and a supply was readily obtained of respectable volunteers, who flocked from all parts of England to support the cause of their political friends. The new parliament opened with the victory of an opposition, which was fortified by strong clamour and strange coalitions. From the event of the first divisions, Sir Robert Walpole perceived that he could no longer lead a majority in the House of Commons, and prudently resigned (after a dominion of one-and-twenty years) the guidance of the state (1742). But the fall of an unpopular minister was not succeeded, according to general expectation, by a millennium of happiness and virtue: some courtiers lost their places, some patriots lost their characters, Lord Orford's offences vanished with his power; and after a short vibration, the Pelham government was fixed on the old basis of the Whig aristocracy. In the year 1745, the throne and the constitution were attacked by a rebellion, which does not reflect much honour on the national spirit; since the English friends of the Pretender wanted courage to join his standard, and his enemies (the bulk of the people) allowed him to advance into the heart of the kingdom. Without daring, perhaps without desiring, to aid the rebels, my father invariably adhered to the Tory opposition. In the most critical season he accepted, for the service of the party, the office of alderman in the city of London: but the duties were so repugnant to his inclination and habits, that he resigned his gown at the end of a few months. The second parliament in which he sat was prematurely dissolved (1747): and as he was unable or unwilling to maintain a second contest for Southampton, the life of the senator expired in that dissolution.

The death of a new-born child before that of its parents may seem an unnatural, but it is strictly a probable, event: since of any given number the greater part are extinguished before their ninth year, before they possess the faculties of the mind or body. Without accusing the profuse waste or imperfect workmanship of Nature, I shall only observe, that this unfavourable chance was multiplied against my infant existence. So feeble was my constitution, so precarious my life, that, in the baptism of each of my brothers, my father's prudence successively repeated my Christian name of Edward, that, in case of the departure of the eldest son, this patronymic appellation might be still perpetuated in the family.

—Uno avulso non deficit alter.

To preserve and to rear so frail a being, the most tender assiduity was scarcely sufficient, and my mother's attention was somewhat diverted by an exclusive passion for her husband, and by the dissipation of the world, in which his taste and authority obliged her to mingle. But the maternal office was supplied by my aunt, Mrs. Catherine Porten; at whose name I feel a tear of gratitude trickling down my cheek. A life of celibacy transferred her vacant affection to her sister's first child; my weakness excited her pity; her attachment was fortified by labour and success: and if there be any, as I trust there are some, who rejoice that I live, to that dear and excellent woman they must hold themselves indebted. Many anxious and solitary days did she consume in the patient trial of every mode of relief and amusement. Many wakeful nights did she sit by my bedside in trembling expectation that each hour would be my last. Of the various and frequent disorders of my childhood my own recollection is dark. Suffice it to say, that while every practitioner, from Sloane and Ward to the Chevalier Taylor, was successively summoned to torture or relieve me, the care of my mind was too frequently neglected for that of my health: compassion always suggested an excuse for the indulgence of the master, or the idleness of the pupil; and the chain of my education was broken, as often as I was recalled from the school of learning to the bed of sickness.

As soon as the use of speech had prepared my infant reason for the admission of knowledge, I was taught the arts of reading, writing, and arithmetic. So remote is the date, so vague is the memory of their origin in myself, that, were not the error corrected by analogy, I should be tempted to conceive them as innate. In my childhood I was praised for the readiness with which I could multiply and divide, by memory alone, two sums of several figures; such praise encouraged my growing talent; and had I persevered in this line of application, I might have acquired some fame in mathematical studies.

After this previous institution at home, or at a day school at Putney, I was delivered at the age of seven into the hands of Mr. John Kirkby, who exercised about eighteen months the office of my domestic tutor. His learning and virtue introduced him to my father; and at Putney he might have found at least a temporary shelter, had not an act of indiscretion driven him into the world. One day reading prayers in the parish church, he most unluckily forgot the name of King George: his patron, a loyal subject, dismissed him with some reluctance, and a decent reward; and how the poor man ended his days I have never been able to learn. Mr. John Kirkby is the author of two small volumes; the Life of Automathes (London, 1745), and an English and Latin Grammar (London, 1746); which, as a testimony of gratitude, he dedicated (Nov. 5th, 1745) to my father. The books are before me: from them the pupil may judge the preceptor; and, upon the whole, his judgment will not be unfavourable. The grammar is executed with accuracy and skill, and I know not whether any better existed at the time in our language: but the Life of Automathes aspires to the honours of a philosophical fiction. It is the story of a youth, the son of a ship-wrecked exile, who lives alone on a desert island from infancy to the age of manhood. A hind is his nurse; he inherits a cottage, with many useful and curious instruments; some ideas remain of the education of his two first years; some arts are borrowed from the beavers of a neighbouring lake; some truths are revealed in supernatural visions. With these helps, and his own industry, Automathes becomes a self- taught though speechless philosopher, who had investigated with success his own mind, the natural world, the abstract sciences, and the great principles of morality and religion. The author is not entitled to the merit of invention, since he has blended the English story of Robinson Crusoe with the Arabian romance of Hai Ebn Yokhdan, which he might have read in the Latin version of Pocock. In the Automathes I cannot praise either the depth of thought or elegance of style; but the book is not devoid of entertainment or instruction; and among several interesting passages, I would select the discovery of fire, which produces by accidental mischief the discovery of conscience. A man who had thought so much on the subjects of language and education was surely no ordinary preceptor: my childish years, and his hasty departure, prevented me from enjoying the full benefit of his lessons; but they enlarged my knowledge of arithmetic, and left me a clear impression of the English and Latin rudiments.

In my ninth year (Jan., 1746), in a lucid interval of comparative health, my father adopted the convenient and customary mode of English education; and I was sent to Kingston-upon-Thames, to a school of about seventy boys, which was kept by Dr. Wooddeson and his assistants. Every time I have since passed over Putney Common, I have always noticed the spot where my mother, as we drove along in the coach, admonished me that I was now going into the world, and must learn to think and act for myself. The expression may appear ludicrous; yet there is not, in the course of life, a more remarkable change than the removal of a child from the luxury and freedom of a wealthy house, to the frugal diet and strict subordination of a school; from the tenderness of parents, and the obsequiousness of servants, to the rude familiarity of his equals, the insolent tyranny of his seniors, and the rod, perhaps, of a cruel and capricious pedagogue. Such hardships may steel the mind and body against the injuries of fortune; but my timid reserve was astonished by the crowd and tumult of the school;

the want of strength and activity disqualified me for the sports of the play-field; nor have I forgotten how often in the year forty-six I was reviled and buffeted for the sins of my Tory ancestors. By the common methods of discipline, at the expence of many tears and some blood, I purchased the knowledge of the Latin syntax: and not long since I was possessed of the dirty volumes of Phaedrus and Cornelius Nepos, which I painfully construed and darkly understood. The choice of these authors is not injudicious. The lives of Cornelius Nepos, the friend of Atticus and Cicero, are composed in the style of the purest age: his simplicity is elegant, his brevity copious; he exhibits a series of men and manners; and with such illustrations, as every pedant is not indeed qualified to give, this classic biographer may initiate a young student in the history of Greece and Rome. The use of fables or apologues has been approved in every age from ancient India to modern Europe. They convey in familiar images the truths of morality and prudence; and the most childish understanding (I advert to the scruples of Rousseau) will not suppose either that beasts do speak, or that men may lie. A fable represents the genuine characters of animals; and a skilful master might extract from Pliny and Buffon some pleasing lessons of natural history, a science well adapted to the taste and capacity of children. The Latinity of Phaedrus is not exempt from an alloy of the silver age; but his manner is concise, terse, and sententious; the Thracian slave discreetly breathes the spirit of a freeman; and when the text is found, the style is perspicuous. But his fables, after a long oblivion, were first published by Peter Pithou, from a corrupt manuscript. The labours of fifty editors confess the defects of the copy, as well as the value of the original; and the school-boy may have been whipped for misapprehending a passage, which Bentley could not restore, and which Burman could not explain.

My studies were too frequently interrupted by sickness; and after a real or nominal residence at Kingston School of near two years, I was finally recalled (Dec., 1747) by my mother's death, in her thirty-eighth year. I was too young to feel the importance of my loss; and the image of her person and conversation is faintly imprinted in my memory. The affectionate heart of my aunt, Catherine Porten, bewailed a sister and a friend; but my poor father was inconsolable, and the transport of grief seemed to threaten his life or his reason.

I can never forget the scene of our first interview, some weeks after the fatal event; the awful silence, the room hung with black, the mid-day tapers, his sighs and tears; his praises of my mother, a saint in heaven; his solemn adjuration that I would cherish her memory and imitate her virtues; and the fervor with which he kissed and blessed me as the sole surviving pledge of their loves. The storm of passion insensibly subsided into calmer melancholy. At a convivial meeting of his friends, Mr. Gibbon might affect or enjoy a gleam of cheerfulness; but his plan of happiness was for ever destroyed: and after the loss of his companion he was left alone in a world, of which the business and pleasures were to him irksome or insipid. After some unsuccessful trials he renounced the tumult of London and the hospitality of Putney, and buried himself in the rural or rather rustic solitude of Beriton; from which, during several years, he seldom emerged.

As far back as I can remember, the house, near Putney-bridge and churchyard, of my maternal grandfather appears in the light of my proper and native home. It was there that I was allowed to spend the greatest part of my time, in sickness or in health, during my school vacations and my parents' residence in London, and finally after my mother's death. Three months after that event, in the spring of 1748, the commercial ruin of her father, Mr. James Porten, was accomplished and declared. He suddenly absconded: but as his effects were not sold, nor the house evacuated, till the Christmas following, I enjoyed during the whole year the society of my aunt, without much consciousness of her impending fate. I feel a melancholy pleasure in repeating my obligations to that excellent woman, Mrs. Catherine Porten, the true mother of my mind as well as of my health. Her natural good sense was improved by the perusal of the best books in the English language; and if her reason was sometimes clouded by prejudice, her sentiments were never disguised by hypocrisy or affectation. Her indulgent tenderness, the frankness of her temper, and my innate rising curiosity, soon removed all distance between us: like friends of an equal age, we freely conversed on every topic, familiar or abstruse; and it was her delight and reward to observe the first shoots of my young ideas. Pain and languor were often soothed by the voice of instruction and amusement; and to her kind lessons I ascribe my early and invincible love of reading, which I would not exchange for the treasures of India. I should perhaps be astonished, were it possible to ascertain the date, at which a favourite tale was engraved, by frequent repetition, in my memory: the Cavern of the Winds; the Palace of Felicity; and the fatal moment, at the end of three months or centuries, when Prince Adolphus is overtaken by Time, who had worn out so many pair of wings in the pursuit. Before I left Kingston school I was well acquainted with Pope's Homer and the Arabian Nights Entertainments, two books which will always please by the moving picture of human manners and specious miracles: nor was I then capable of discerning that Pope's translation is a portrait endowed with every merit, excepting that of likeness to the original. The verses of Pope accustomed my ear to the sound of poetic harmony: in the death of Hector, and the shipwreck of Ulysses, I tasted the new emotions of terror and pity; and seriously disputed with my aunt on the vices and virtues of the heroes of the Trojan war. From Pope's Homer to Dryden's Virgil was an easy transition; but I know not how, from some fault in the author, the translator, or the reader, the pious Aeneas did not so forcibly seize on my imagination; and I derived more pleasure from Ovid's Metamorphoses, especially in the fall of Phaeton, and the speeches of Ajax and Ulysses. My grand-father's flight unlocked the door of a tolerable library; and I turned over many English pages of poetry and romance, of history and travels. Where a title attracted my eye, without fear or awe I snatched the volume from the shelf; and Mrs. Porten, who indulged herself in moral and religious speculations, was more prone to encourage than to check a curiosity above the strength of a boy. This year (1748), the twelfth of my age, I shall note as the most propitious to the growth of my intellectual stature.

The relics of my grandfather's fortune afforded a bare annuity for his own maintenance; and his daughter, my worthy aunt, who had already passed her fortieth year, was left destitute. Her noble spirit scorned a life of obligation and dependence; and after revolving several schemes, she preferred the humble industry of keeping a boarding-house for Westminster-school, where she laboriously earned a competence for her old age. This singular opportunity of blending the advantages of private and public education decided my father. After the Christmas holidays in January, 1749, I accompanied Mrs. Porten to her new house in

College-street; and was immediately entered in the school of which Dr. John Nicoll was at that time head-master. At first I was alone: but my aunt's resolution was praised; her character was esteemed; her friends were numerous and active: in the course of some years she became the mother of forty or fifty boys, for the most part of family and fortune; and as her primitive habitation was too narrow, she built and occupied a spacious mansion in Dean's Yard. I shall always be ready to join in the common opinion that our public schools, which have produced so many eminent characters, are the best adapted to the genius and constitution of the English people. A boy of spirit may acquire a previous and practical experience of the world; and his playfellows may be the future friends of his heart or his interest. In a free intercourse with his equals, the habits of truth, fortitude, and prudence will insensibly be matured. Birth and riches are measured by the standard of personal merit; and the mimic scene of a rebellion has displayed, in their true colours, the ministers and patriots of the rising generation. Our seminaries of learning do not exactly correspond with the precept of a Spartan king, "that the child should be instructed in the arts, which will be useful to the man;" since a finished scholar may emerge from the head of Westminster or Eton, in total ignorance of the business and conversation of English gentlemen in the latter end of the eighteenth century. But these schools may assume the merit of teaching all that they pretend to teach, the Latin and Greek languages: they deposit in the hands of a disciple the keys of two valuable chests; nor can he complain, if they are afterwards lost or neglected by his own fault. The necessity of leading in equal ranks so many unequal powers of capacity and application, will prolong to eight or ten years the juvenile studies, which might be despatched in half that time by the skilful master of a single pupil. Yet even the repetition of exercise and discipline contributes to fix in a vacant mind the verbal science of grammar and prosody: and the private or voluntary student, who possesses the sense and spirit of the classics, may offend, by a false quantity, the scrupulous ear of a well-flogged critic. For myself, I must be content with a very small share of the civil and literary fruits of a public school. In the space of two years (1749, 1750), interrupted by danger and debility, I painfully climbed into the third form; and my riper age was left to acquire the beauties of the Latin, and the rudiments of the Greek tongue. Instead of audaciously mingling in the sports, the quarrels, and the connections of our little world, I was still cherished at home under the maternal wing of my aunt; and my removal from Westminster long preceded the approach of manhood.

The violence and variety of my complaint, which had excused my frequent absence from Westminster School, at length engaged Mrs. Porten, with the advice of physicians, to conduct me to Bath: at the end of the Michaelmas vacation (1750) she quitted me with reluctance, and I remained several months under the care of a trusty maid-servant. A strange nervous affection, which alternately contracted my legs, and produced, without any visible symptoms, the most excruciating pain, was ineffectually opposed by the various methods of bathing and pumping. From Bath I was transported to Winchester, to the house of a physician; and after the failure of his medical skill, we had again recourse to the virtues of the Bath waters. During the intervals of these fits, I moved with my father to Beriton and Putney; and a short unsuccessful trial was attempted to renew my attendance at Westminster School. But my infirmities could not be reconciled with the hours and discipline of a public seminary; and instead of a domestic tutor, who might have watched the favourable moments, and gently advanced the progress of my learning, my father was too easily content with such occasional teachers as the different places of my residence could supply. I was never forced, and seldom was I persuaded, to admit these lessons: yet I read with a clergyman at Bath some odes of Horace, and several episodes of Virgil, which gave me an imperfect and transient enjoyment of the Latin poets. It might now be apprehended that I should continue for life an illiterate cripple; but, as I approached my sixteenth year, Nature displayed in my favour her mysterious energies: my constitution was fortified and fixed; and my disorders, instead of growing with my growth and strengthening with my strength, most wonderfully vanished. I have never possessed or abused the insolence of health: but since that time few persons have been more exempt from real or imaginary ills; and, till I am admonished by the gout, the reader will no more be troubled with the history of my bodily complaints. My unexpected recovery again encouraged the hope of my education; and I was placed at Esher, in Surrey, in the house of the Reverend Mr. Philip Francis, in a pleasant spot, which promised to unite the various benefits of air, exercise, and study (Jan.,1752). The translator of Horace might have taught me to relish the Latin poets, had not my friends discovered in a few weeks, that he preferred the pleasures of London, to the instruction of his pupils. My father's perplexity at this time, rather than his prudence, was urged to embrace a singular and desperate measure. Without preparation or delay he carried me to Oxford; and I was matriculated in the university as a gentleman commoner of Magdalen college, before I had accomplished the fifteenth year of my age (April 3, 1752).

The curiosity, which had been implanted in my infant mind, was still alive and active; but my reason was not sufficiently informed to understand the value, or to lament the loss, of three precious years from my entrance at Westminster to my admission at Oxford. Instead of repining at my long and frequent confinement to the chamber or the couch, I secretly rejoiced in those infirmities, which delivered me from the exercises of the school, and the society of my equals. As often as I was tolerably exempt from danger and pain, reading, free desultory reading, was the employment and comfort of my solitary hours. At Westminster, my aunt sought only to amuse and indulge me; in my stations at Bath and Winchester, at Beriton and Putney, a false compassion respected my sufferings; and I was allowed, without controul or advice, to gratify the wanderings of an unripe taste. My indiscriminate appetite subsided by degrees in the historic line: and since philosophy has exploded all innate ideas and natural propensities, I must ascribe this choice to the assiduous perusal of the Universal History, as the octavo volumes successively appeared. This unequal work, and a treatise of Hearne, the Ductor historicus, referred and introduced me to the Greek and Roman historians, to as many at least as were accessible to an English reader. All that I could find were greedily devoured, from Littlebury's lame Herodotus, and Spelman's valuable Xenophon, to the pompous folios of Gordon's Tacitus, and a ragged Procopius of the beginning of the last century. The cheap acquisition of so much knowledge confirmed my dislike to the study of languages; and I argued with Mrs. Porten, that, were I master of Greek and Latin, I must interpret to myself in English the thoughts of the original, and that such extemporary versions must be inferior to the elaborate translations of professed scholars; a silly sophism, which could not easily be confuted by a person ignorant of any other language than her own. From the ancient I leaped to the modern world: many crude lumps of Speed, Rapin, Mezeray, Davila, Machiavel, Father Paul, Bower, &c., I devoured like so many novels; and I swallowed with the same voracious appetite the descriptions of India and China, of Mexico and Peru.

My first introduction to the historic scenes, which have since engaged so many years of my life, must be ascribed to an accident. In the summer of 1751, I accompanied my father on a visit to Mr. Hoare's, in Wiltshire; but I was less delighted with the beauties of Stourhead, than with discovering in the library a common book, the Continuation of Echard's Roman History, which is indeed executed with more skill and taste than the previous work. To me the reigns of the successors of Constantine were absolutely new; and I was immersed in the passage of the Goths over the Danube, when the summons of the dinner-bell reluctantly dragged me from my intellectual feast. This transient glance served rather to irritate than to appease my curiosity; and as soon as I returned to Bath I procured the second and third volumes of Howel's History of the World, which exhibit the Byzantine period on a larger scale. Mahomet and his Saracens soon fixed my attention; and some instinct of criticism directed me to the genuine sources. Simon Ockley, an original in every sense, first opened my eyes; and I was led from one book to another, till I had ranged round the circle of Oriental history. Before I was sixteen, I had exhausted all that could be learned in English of the Arabs and Persians, the Tartars and Turks; and the same ardour urged me to guess at the French of D'Herbelot, and to construe the barbarous Latin of Pocock's Abulfaragius. Such vague and multifarious reading could not teach me to think, to write, or to act; and the only principle that darted a ray of light into the indigested chaos, was an early and rational application to the order of time and place. The maps of Cellarius and Wells imprinted in my mind the picture of ancient geography: from Stranchius I imbibed the elements of chronology: the Tables of Helvicus and Anderson, the Annals of Usher and Prideaux, distinguished the connection of events, and engraved the multitude of names and dates in a clear and indelible series. But in the discussion of the first ages I overleaped the bounds of modesty and use. In my childish balance I presumed to weigh the systems of Scaliger and Petavius, of Marsham and Newton, which I could seldom study in the originals; and my sleep has been disturbed by the difficulty of reconciling the Septuagint with the Hebrew computation. I arrived at Oxford with a stock of erudition, that might have puzzled a doctor, and a degree of ignorance, of which a school-boy would have been ashamed.

At the conclusion of this first period of my life, I am tempted to enter a protest against the trite and lavish praise of the happiness of our boyish years, which is echoed with so much affectation in the world. That happiness I have never known, that time I have never regretted; and were my poor aunt still alive, she would bear testimony to the early and constant uniformity of my sentiments. It will indeed be replied, that I am not a competent judge; that pleasure is incompatible with pain; that joy is excluded from sickness; and that the felicity of a schoolboy consists in the perpetual motion of thoughtless and playful agility, in which I was never qualified to excel. My name, it is most true, could never be enrolled among the sprightly race, the idle progeny of Eton or Westminster,

"Who foremost may delight to cleave,
With pliant arm, the glassy wave,
Or urge the flying ball."

The poet may gaily describe the short hours of recreation; but he forgets the daily tedious labours of the school, which is approached each morning with anxious and reluctant steps.

A traveller, who visits Oxford or Cambridge, is surprised and edified by the apparent order and tranquillity that prevail in the seats of the English muses. In the most celebrated universities of Holland, Germany, and Italy, the students, who swarm from different countries, are loosely dispersed in private lodgings at the houses of the burghers: they dress according to their fancy and fortune; and in the intemperate quarrels of youth and wine, their swords, though less frequently than of old, are sometimes stained with each other's blood. The use of arms is banished from our English universities; the uniform habit of the academics, the square cap, and black gown, is adapted to the civil and even clerical profession; and from the doctor in divinity to the under-graduate, the degrees of learning and age are externally distinguished. Instead of being scattered in a town, the students of Oxford and Cambridge are united in colleges; their maintenance is provided at their own expense, or that of the founders; and the stated hours of the hall and chapel represent the discipline of a regular, and, as it were, a religious community. The eyes of the traveller are attracted by the size or beauty of the public edifices; and the principal colleges appear to be so many palaces, which a liberal nation has erected and endowed for the habitation of science. My own introduction to the university of Oxford forms a new aera in my life; and at the distance of forty years I still remember my first emotions of surprise and satisfaction. In my fifteenth year I felt myself suddenly raised from a boy to a man: the persons, whom I respected as my superiors in age and academical rank, entertained me with every mark of attention and civility; and my vanity was flattered by the velvet cap and silk gown, which distinguish a gentleman commoner from a plebeian student. A decent allowance, more money than a schoolboy had ever seen, was at my own disposal; and I might command, among the tradesmen of Oxford, an indefinite and dangerous latitude of credit. A key was delivered into my hands, which gave me the free use of a numerous and learned library; my apartment consisted of three elegant and well-furnished rooms in the new building, a stately pile, of Magdalen College; and the adjacent walks, had they been frequented by Plato's disciples, might have been compared to the Attic shade on the banks of the Ilissus. Such was the fair prospect of my entrance (April 3, 1752) into the university of Oxford.

A venerable prelate, whose taste and erudition must reflect honour on the society in which they were formed, has drawn a very interesting picture of his academical life.—"I was educated (says Bishop Lowth) in the UNIVERSITY OF OXFORD. I enjoyed all the advantages, both public and private, which that famous seat of learning so largely affords. I spent many years in that illustrious society, in a well-regulated course of useful discipline and studies, and in the agreeable and improving commerce of gentlemen and of scholars; in a society where emulation without envy, ambition without jealousy, contention without animosity, incited industry, and awakened genius; where a liberal pursuit of knowledge, and a genuine freedom of thought, were raised, encouraged, and pushed forward by example, by commendation, and by authority. I breathed the same atmosphere that the HOOKERS, the CHILLINGWORTHS, and the LOCKES had breathed before; whose benevolence and humanity were as extensive as their vast genius and comprehensive knowledge; who always treated their adversaries with civility and respect; who made candour, moderation, and liberal judgment as much the rule and law as the subject of their discourse. And do you reproach me with my education in this place, and with my relation to this most respectable body, which I shall always esteem my greatest advantage and my highest honour?" I transcribe with pleasure this eloquent passage, without examining what benefits or what rewards were derived by Hooker, or Chillingworth, or Locke, from their academical institution; without inquiring, whether in this angry controversy the spirit of Lowth himself is purified from the intolerant zeal, which Warburton had ascribed to the genius of the place. It may indeed be observed, that the atmosphere of Oxford did not agree with Mr. Locke's constitution; and that the philosopher justly despised the academical bigots, who expelled his person and condemned his principles. The expression of gratitude is a virtue and a pleasure: a liberal mind will delight to cherish and celebrate the memory of its parents; and the teachers of science are the parents of the mind. I applaud the filial piety, which it is impossible for me to imitate; since I must not confess an imaginary debt, to assume the merit of a just or generous retribution. To the university of Oxford I acknowledge no obligation; and she will as cheerfully renounce me for a son, as I am willing to disclaim her for a mother. I spent fourteen months at Magdalen College; they proved the fourteen months the most idle and unprofitable of my whole life: the reader will pronounce between the school and the scholar; but I cannot affect to believe that Nature had disqualified me for all literary pursuits. The specious and ready excuse of my tender age, imperfect preparation, and hasty departure, may doubtless be alleged; nor do I wish to defraud such excuses of their proper weight. Yet in my sixteenth year I was not devoid of capacity or application; even my childish reading had displayed an early though blind propensity for books; and the shallow flood might have been taught to flow in a deep channel and a clear stream. In the discipline of a well-constituted academy, under the guidance of skilful and vigilant professors, I should gradually have risen from translations to originals, from the Latin to the Greek classics, from dead languages to living science: my hours would have been occupied by useful and agreeable studies, the wanderings of fancy would have been restrained, and I should have escaped the temptations of idleness, which finally precipitated my departure from Oxford.

Perhaps in a separate annotation I may coolly examine the fabulous and real antiquities of our sister universities, a question which has kindled such fierce and foolish disputes among their fanatic sons. In the meanwhile it will be acknowledged that these venerable bodies are sufficiently old to partake of all the prejudices and infirmities of age. The schools of Oxford and Cambridge were founded in a dark age of false and barbarous science; and they are still tainted with the vices of their origin. Their primitive discipline was adapted to the education of priests and monks; and the government still remains in the hands of the clergy, an order of men whose manners are remote from the present world, and whose eyes are dazzled by the light of philosophy. The legal incorporation of these societies by the charters of popes and kings had given them a monopoly of the public instruction; and the spirit of monopolists is narrow, lazy, and oppressive; their work is more costly and less productive than that of independent artists; and the new improvements so eagerly grasped by the competition of freedom, are admitted with slow and sullen reluctance in those proud corporations, above the fear of a rival, and below the confession of an error. We may scarcely hope that any reformation will be a voluntary act; and so deeply are they rooted in law and prejudice, that even the omnipotence of parliament would shrink from an inquiry into the state and abuses of the two universities.

The use of academical degrees, as old as the thirteenth century, is visibly borrowed from the mechanic corporations; in which an apprentice, after serving his time, obtains a testimonial of his skill, and a licence to practise his trade and mystery. It is not my design to depreciate those honours, which could never gratify or disappoint my ambition; and I should applaud the institution, if the degrees of bachelor or licentiate were bestowed as the reward of manly and successful study: if the name and rank of doctor or master were strictly reserved for the professors of science, who have approved their title to the public esteem.

In all the universities of Europe, excepting our own, the languages and sciences are distributed among a numerous list of effective professors: the students, according to their taste, their calling, and their diligence, apply themselves to the proper masters; and in the annual repetition of public and private lectures, these masters are assiduously employed. Our curiosity may inquire what number of professors has been instituted at Oxford? (for I shall now confine myself to my own university;) by whom are they appointed, and what may be the probable chances of merit or incapacity; how many are stationed to the three faculties, and how many are left for the liberal arts? what is the form, and what the substance, of their lessons? But all these questions are silenced by one short and singular answer, "That in the University of Oxford, the greater part of the public professors have for these many years given up altogether even the pretence of teaching." Incredible as the fact may appear, I must rest my belief on the positive and impartial evidence of a master of moral and political wisdom, who had himself resided at Oxford. Dr. Adam Smith assigns as the cause of their indolence, that, instead of being paid by voluntary contributions, which would urge them to increase the number, and to deserve the gratitude of their pupils, the Oxford professors are secure in the enjoyment of a fixed stipend, without the necessity of labour, or the apprehension of controul. It has indeed been observed, nor is the observation absurd, that excepting in experimental sciences, which demand a costly apparatus and a dexterous hand, the many valuable treatises, that have been published on every subject of learning, may now supersede the ancient mode of oral instruction. Were this principle true in its utmost latitude, I should only infer that the offices and salaries, which are become useless, ought without delay to be abolished. But there still remains a material difference between a book and a professor; the hour of the lecture enforces attendance; attention is fixed by the presence, the voice, and the occasional questions of the teacher; the most idle will carry something away; and the more diligent will compare the instructions, which they have heard in the school, with the volumes, which they peruse in their chamber. The advice of a skilful professor will adapt a course of reading to every mind and every situation; his authority will discover, admonish, and at last chastise the negligence of his disciples; and his vigilant inquiries will ascertain the steps of their literary progress. Whatever science he professes he may illustrate in a series of discourses, composed in the leisure of his closet, pronounced on public occasions, and finally delivered to the press. I observe with pleasure, that in the university of Oxford Dr. Lowth, with equal eloquence and erudition, has executed this task in his incomparable Praelections on the Poetry of the Hebrews.

The college of St. Mary Magdalen was founded in the fifteenth century by Wainfleet, bishop of Winchester; and now consists of a president, forty fellows, and a number of inferior students. It is esteemed one of the largest and most wealthy of our academical corporations, which may be compared to the Benedictine abbeys of Catholic countries; and I have loosely heard that the estates belonging to Magdalen College, which are leased by those indulgent landlords at small quit-rents and occasional fines, might be raised, in the hands of private avarice, to an annual revenue of nearly thirty thousand pounds. Our colleges are supposed to be schools of science, as well as of education; nor is it unreasonable to expect that a body of literary men, devoted to a life of celibacy, exempt from the care of their own subsistence, and amply provided with books, should devote their leisure to the prosecution of study, and that some effects of their studies should be manifested to the world. The shelves of their library groan under the weight of the Benedictine folios, of the editions of the fathers, and the collections of the middle ages, which have issued from the single abbey of St. Germain de Prez at Paris. A composition of genius must be the offspring of one mind; but such works of industry, as may be divided among many hands, and must be continued during many years, are the peculiar province of a laborious community. If I inquire into the manufactures of the monks of Magdalen, if I extend the inquiry to the other colleges of Oxford and Cambridge, a silent blush, or a scornful frown, will be the only reply. The fellows or monks of my time were decent easy men, who supinely enjoyed the gifts of the founder; their days were filled by a series of uniform employments; the chapel and the hall, the coffee-house and the common room, till they retired, weary and well satisfied, to a long slumber. From the toil of reading, or thinking, or writing, they had absolved their conscience; and the first shoots of learning and ingenuity withered on the ground, without yielding any fruits to the owners or the public. As a gentleman commoner, I was admitted to the society of the fellows, and fondly expected that some questions of literature would be the amusing and instructive topics of their discourse.

Their conversation stagnated in a round of college business, Tory politics, personal anecdotes, and private scandal: their dull and deep potations excused the brisk intemperance of youth; and their constitutional toasts were not expressive of the most lively loyalty for the house of Hanover. A general election was now approaching: the great Oxfordshire contest already blazed with all the malevolence of party-zeal. Magdalen College was devoutly attached to the old interest! and the names of Wenman and Dashwood were more frequently pronounced, than those of Cicero and Chrysostom. The example of the senior fellows could not inspire the under-graduates with a liberal spirit or studious emulation; and I cannot describe, as I never knew, the discipline of college. Some duties may possibly have been imposed on the poor scholars, whose ambition aspired to the peaceful honours of a fellowship (ascribi quietis ordinibus—Deorum); but no independent members were admitted below the rank of a gentleman commoner, and our velvet cap was the cap of liberty. A tradition prevailed that some of our predecessors had spoken Latin declamations in the hall; but of this ancient custom no vestige remained: the obvious methods of public exercises and examinations were totally unknown; and I have never heard that either the president or the society interfered in the private economy of the tutors and their pupils.

The silence of the Oxford professors, which deprives the youth of public instruction, is imperfectly supplied by the tutors, as they are styled, of the several colleges. Instead of confining themselves to a single science, which had satisfied the ambition of Burman or Bernoulli, they teach, or promise to teach, either history or mathematics, or ancient literature, or moral philosophy; and as it is possible that they may be defective in all, it is highly probable that of some they will be ignorant. They are paid, indeed, by voluntary contributions; but their appointment depends on the head of the house: their diligence is voluntary, and will consequently be languid, while the pupils themselves, or their parents, are not indulged in the liberty of choice or change. The first tutor into whose hands I was resigned appears to have been one of the best of the tribe: Dr. Waldegrave was a learned and pious man, of a mild disposition, strict morals, and abstemious life, who seldom mingled in the politics or the jollity of the college. But his knowledge of the world was confined to the university; his learning was of the last, rather than the present age; his temper was indolent; his faculties, which were not of the first rate, had been relaxed by the climate, and he was satisfied, like his fellows, with the slight and superficial discharge of an important trust. As soon as my tutor had sounded the insufficiency of his pupil in school-learning, he proposed that we should read every morning from ten to eleven the comedies of Terence. The sum of my improvement in the university of Oxford is confined to three or four Latin plays; and even the study of an elegant classic, which might have been illustrated by a comparison of ancient and modern theatres, was reduced to a dry and literal interpretation of the author's text. During the first weeks I constantly attended these lessons in my tutor's room; but as they appeared equally devoid of profit and pleasure I was once tempted to try the experiment of a formal apology. The apology was accepted with a smile. I repeated the offence with less ceremony; the excuse was admitted with the same indulgence: the slightest motive of laziness or indisposition, the most trifling avocation at home or abroad, was allowed as a worthy impediment; nor did my tutor appear conscious of my absence or neglect. Had the hour of lecture been constantly filled, a single hour was a small portion of my academic leisure. No plan of study was recommended for my use; no exercises were prescribed for his inspection; and, at the most precious season of youth, whole days and weeks were suffered to elapse without labour or amusement, without advice or account. I should have listened to the voice of reason and of my tutor; his mild behaviour had gained my confidence. I preferred his society to that of the younger students; and in our evening walks to the top of Heddington-hill, we freely conversed on a variety of subjects. Since the days of Pocock and Hyde, Oriental learning has always been the pride of Oxford, and I once expressed an inclination to study Arabic. His prudence discouraged this childish fancy; but he neglected the fair occasion of directing the ardour of a curious mind. During my absence in the summer vacation, Dr. Waldegrave accepted a college living at Washington in Sussex, and on my return I no longer found him at Oxford. From that time I have lost sight of my first tutor; but at the end of thirty years (1781) he was still alive; and the practice of exercise and temperance had entitled him to a healthy old age.

The long recess between the Trinity and Michaelmas terms empties the colleges of Oxford, as well as the courts of Westminster. I spent, at my father's house at Beriton in Hampshire, the two months of August and September. It is whimsical enough, that as soon as I left Magdalen College, my taste for books began to revive; but it was the same blind and boyish taste for the pursuit of exotic history. Unprovided with original learning, unformed in the habits of thinking, unskilled in the arts of composition, I resolved to write a book. The title of this first Essay, The Age of Sesostris, was perhaps suggested by Voltaire's Age of Lewis XIV. which was new and popular; but my sole object was to investigate the probable date of the life and reign of the conqueror of Asia. I was then enamoured of Sir John Marsham's Canon Chronicus; an elaborate work, of whose merits and defects I was not yet qualified to judge. According to his specious, though narrow plan, I settled my hero about the time of Solomon, in the tenth century before the Christian era. It was therefore incumbent on me, unless I would adopt Sir Isaac Newton's shorter chronology, to remove a formidable objection; and my solution, for a youth of fifteen, is not devoid of ingenuity. In his version of the Sacred Books, Manetho, high priest has identified Sethosis, or Sesostris, with the elder brother of Danaus, who landed in Greece, according to the Parian Marble, fifteen hundred and ten years before Christ. But in my supposition the high priest is guilty of a voluntary error; flattery is the prolific parent of falsehood. Manetho's History of Egypt is dedicated to Ptolemy Philadelphus, who derived a fabulous or illegitimate pedigree from the Macedonian kings of the race of Hercules. Danaus is the ancestor of Hercules; and after the failure of the elder branch, his descendants, the Ptolemies, are the sole representatives of the royal family, and may claim by inheritance the kingdom which they hold by conquest. Such were my juvenile discoveries; at a riper age I no longer presume to connect the Greek, the Jewish, and the Egyptian antiquities, which are lost in a distant cloud. Nor is this the only instance, in which the belief and knowledge of the child are superseded by the more rational ignorance of the man. During my stay at Beriton, my infant-labour was diligently prosecuted, without much interruption from company or country diversions; and I already heard the music of public applause. The discovery of my own weakness was the first symptom of taste. On my return to Oxford, the Age of Sesostris was wisely relinquished; but the imperfect sheets remained twenty years at the bottom of a drawer, till, in a general clearance of papers (Nov., 1772,) they were committed to the flames.

After the departure of Dr. Waldegrave, I was transferred, with his other pupils, to his academical heir, whose literary character did not command the respect of the college. Dr—well remembered that he had a salary to receive, and only forgot that he had a duty to perform. Instead of guiding the studies, and watching over the behaviour of his disciple, I was never summoned to attend even the ceremony of a lecture; and, excepting one voluntary visit to his rooms, during the eight months of his titular office, the tutor and pupil lived in the same college as strangers to each other. The want of experience, of advice, and of occupation, soon betrayed me into some improprieties of conduct, ill-chosen company, late hours, and inconsiderate expense. My growing debts might be secret; but my frequent absence was visible and scandalous: and a tour to Bath, a visit into Buckingham-shire, and four excursions to London in the same winter, were costly and dangerous frolics. They were, indeed, without a meaning, as without an excuse. The irksomeness of a cloistered life repeatedly tempted me to wander; but my chief pleasure was that of travelling; and I was too young and bashful to enjoy, like a Manly Oxonian in Town, the pleasures of London. In all these excursions I eloped from Oxford; I returned to college; in a few days I eloped again, as if I had been an independent stranger in a hired lodging, without once hearing the voice of admonition, without once feeling the hand of control. Yet my time was lost, my expenses were multiplied, my behaviour abroad was unknown; folly as well as vice should have awakened the attention of my superiors, and my tender years would have justified a more than ordinary degree of restraint and discipline.

It might at least be expected, that an ecclesiastical school should inculcate the orthodox principles of religion. But our venerable mother had contrived to unite the opposite extremes of bigotry and indifference: an heretic, or unbeliever, was a monster in her eyes; but she was always, or often, or sometimes, remiss in the spiritual education of her own children. According to the statutes of the university, every student, before he is matriculated, must subscribe his assent to the thirty-nine articles of the church of England, which are signed by more than read, and read by more than believe them. My insufficient age excused me, however, from the immediate performance of this legal ceremony; and the vice-chancellor directed me to return, as soon as I should have accomplished my fifteenth year; recommending me, in the mean while, to the instruction of my college. My college forgot to instruct: I forgot to return, and was myself forgotten by the first magistrate of the university. Without a single lecture, either public or private, either christian or protestant, without any academical subscription, without any episcopal confirmation, I was left by the dim light of my catechism to grope my way to the chapel and communion-table, where I was admitted, without a question, how far, or by what means, I might be qualified to receive the sacrament. Such almost incredible neglect was productive of the worst mischiefs. From my childhood I had been fond of religious disputation: my poor aunt has been often puzzled by the mysteries which she strove to believe; nor had the elastic spring been totally broken by the weight of the atmosphere of Oxford. The blind activity of idleness urged me to advance without armour into the dangerous mazes of controversy; and at the age of sixteen, I bewildered myself in the errors of the church of Rome.

The progress of my conversion may tend to illustrate, at least, the history of my own mind. It was not long since Dr. Middleton's free inquiry had founded an alarm in the theological world: much ink and much gall had been spilt in the defence of the primitive miracles; and the two dullest of their champions were crowned with academic honours by the university of Oxford. The name of Middleton was unpopular; and his proscription very naturally led me to peruse his writings, and those of his antagonists. His bold criticism, which approaches the precipice of infidelity, produced on my mind a singular effect; and had I persevered in the communion of Rome, I should now apply to my own fortune the prediction of the Sibyl,

—Via prima salutis,
Quod minime reris, Graia, pandetur ab urbe.

The elegance of style and freedom of argument were repelled by a shield of prejudice. I still revered the character, or rather the

41

names, of the saints and fathers whom Dr. Middleton exposes; nor could he destroy my implicit belief, that the gift of miraculous powers was continued in the church, during the first four or five centuries of Christianity. But I was unable to resist the weight of historical evidence, that within the same period most of the leading doctrines of popery were already introduced in theory and practice: nor was my conclusion absurd, that miracles are the test of truth, and that the church must be orthodox and pure, which was so often approved by the visible interposition of the Deity. The marvellous tales which are so boldly attested by the Basils and Chrysostoms, the Austins and Jeroms, compelled me to embrace the superior merits of celibacy, the institution of the monastic life, the use of the sign of the cross, of holy oil, and even of images, the invocation of saints, the worship of relics, the rudiments of purgatory in prayers for the dead, and the tremendous mystery of the sacrifice of the body and blood of Christ, which insensibly swelled into the prodigy of transubstantiation. In these dispositions, and already more than half a convert, I formed an unlucky intimacy with a young gentleman of our college, whose name I shall spare. With a character less resolute, Mr.——had imbibed the same religious opinions; and some Popish books, I know not through what channel, were conveyed into his possession. I read, I applauded, I believed the English translations of two famous works of Bossuet, Bishop of Meaux, the Exposition of the Catholic Doctrine, and the History of the Protestant Variations, achieved my conversion, and I surely fell by a noble hand. I have since examined the originals with a more discerning eye, and shall not hesitate to pronounce, that Bossuet is indeed a master of all the weapons of controversy. In the Exposition, a specious apology, the orator assumes, with consummate art, the tone of candour and simplicity; and the ten-horned monster is transformed, at his magic touch, into the milk-white hind, who must be loved as soon as she is seen. In the History, a bold and well-aimed attack, he displays, with a happy mixture of narrative and argument, the faults and follies, the changes and contradictions of our first reformers; whose variations (as he dexterously contends) are the mark of historical error, while the perpetual unity of the catholic church is the sign and test of infallible truth. To my present feelings it seems incredible that I should ever believe that I believed in transubstantiation. But my conqueror oppressed me with the sacramental words, "Hoc est corpus meum," and dashed against each other the figurative half-meanings of the protestant sects: every objection was resolved into omnipotence; and after repeating at St. Mary's the Athanasian creed, I humbly acquiesced in the mystery of the real presence.

> "To take up half on trust, and half to try,
> Name it not faith, but bungling bigotry,
> Both knave and fool, the merchant we may call,
> To pay great sums, and to compound the small,
> For who would break with Heaven, and would not break
>   for all?"

No sooner had I settled my new religion than I resolved to profess myself a catholic. Youth is sincere and impetuous; and a momentary glow of enthusiasm had raised me above all temporal considerations.

By the keen protestants, who would gladly retaliate the example of persecution, a clamour is raised of the increase of popery: and they are always loud to declaim against the toleration of priests and jesuits, who pervert so many of his majesty's subjects from their religion and allegiance. On the present occasion, the fall of one or more of her sons directed this clamour against the university: and it was confidently affirmed that popish missionaries were suffered, under various disguises, to introduce themselves into the colleges of Oxford. But justice obliges me to declare, that, as far as relates to myself, this assertion is false; and that I never conversed with a priest, or even with a papist, till my resolution from books was absolutely fixed. In my last excursion to London, I addressed myself to Mr. Lewis, a Roman catholic bookseller in Russell-street, Covent Garden, who recommended me to a priest, of whose name and order I am at present ignorant. In our first interview he soon discovered that persuasion was needless. After sounding the motives and merits of my conversion he consented to admit me into the pale of the church; and at his feet on the eighth of June 1753, I solemnly, though privately, abjured the errors of heresy. The seduction of an English youth of family and fortune was an act of as much danger as glory; but he bravely overlooked the danger, of which I was not then sufficiently informed. "Where a person is reconciled to the see of Rome, or procures others to be reconciled, the offence (says Blackstone) amounts to high treason." And if the humanity of the age would prevent the execution of this sanguinary statute, there were other laws of a less odious cast, which condemned the priest to perpetual imprisonment, and transferred the proselyte's estate to his nearest relation. An elaborate controversial epistle, approved by my director, and addressed to my father, announced and justified the step which I had taken. My father was neither a bigot nor a philosopher; but his affection deplored the loss of an only son; and his good sense was astonished at my strange departure from the religion of my country. In the first sally of passion he divulged a secret which prudence might have suppressed, and the gates of Magdalen College were for ever shut against my return. Many years afterwards, when the name of Gibbon was become as notorious as that of Middleton, it was industriously whispered at Oxford, that the historian had formerly "turned papist;" my character stood exposed to the reproach of inconstancy; and this invidious topic would have been handled without mercy by my opponents, could they have separated my cause from that of the university. For my own part, I am proud of an honest sacrifice of interest to conscience. I can never blush, if my tender mind was entangled in the sophistry that seduced the acute and manly understandings of CHILLINGWORTH and BAYLE, who afterwards emerged from superstition to scepticism.

While Charles the First governed England, and was himself governed by a catholic queen, it cannot be denied that the missionaries of Rome laboured with impunity and success in the court, the country, and even the universities. One of the sheep,

—Whom the grim wolf with privy paw
Daily devours apace, and nothing said,

is Mr. William Chillingworth, Master of Arts, and Fellow of Trinity College, Oxford; who, at the ripe age of twenty-eight years, was persuaded to elope from Oxford, to the English seminary at Douay in Flanders. Some disputes with Fisher, a subtle jesuit, might first awaken him from the prejudices of education; but he yielded to his own victorious argument, "that there must be somewhere an infallible judge; and that the church of Rome is the only Christian society which either does or can pretend to that character." After a short trial of a few months, Mr. Chillingworth was again tormented by religious scruples: he returned home, resumed his studies, unravelled his mistakes, and delivered his mind from the yoke of authority and superstition. His new creed was built on the principle, that the Bible is our sole judge, and private reason our sole interpreter: and he ably maintains this principle in the Religion of a Protestant, a book which, after startling the doctors of Oxford, is still esteemed the most solid defence of the Reformation. The learning, the virtue, the recent merits of the author, entitled him to fair preferment: but the slave had now broken his fetters; and the more he weighed, the less was he disposed to subscribe to the thirty-nine articles of the church of England. In a private letter he declares, with all the energy of language, that he could not subscribe to them without subscribing to his own damnation; and that if ever he should depart from this immoveable resolution, he would allow his friends to think him a madman, or an atheist. As the letter is without a date, we cannot ascertain the number of weeks or months that elapsed between this passionate abhorrence and the Salisbury Register, which is still extant. "Ego Gulielmus Chillingworth, . . . omnibus hisce articulis. . . . et singulis in iisdem contentis volens, et ex animo subscribo, et consensum meum iisdem praebeo. 20 die Julii 1638." But, alas! the chancellor and prebendary of Sarum soon deviated from his own subscription: as he more deeply scrutinized the article of the Trinity, neither scripture nor the primitive fathers could long uphold his orthodox belief; and he could not but confess, "that the doctrine of Arius is either the truth, or at least no damnable heresy." From this middle region of the air, the descent of his reason would naturally rest on the firmer ground of the Socinians: and if we may credit a doubtful story, and the popular opinion, his anxious inquiries at last subsided in philosophic indifference. So conspicuous, however, were the candour of his nature and the innocence of his heart, that this apparent levity did not affect the reputation of Chillingworth. His frequent changes proceeded from too nice an inquisition into truth. His doubts grew out of himself; he assisted them with all the strength of his reason: he was then too hard for himself; but finding as little quiet and repose in those victories, he quickly recovered, by a new appeal to his own judgment: so that in all his sallies and retreats, he was in fact his own convert.

Bayle was the son of a Calvinist minister in a remote province of France, at the foot of the Pyrenees. For the benefit of education, the protestants were tempted to risk their children in the catholic universities; and in the twenty-second year of his age, young Bayle was seduced by the arts and arguments of the jesuits of Toulouse. He remained about seventeen months (Mar. 19 1669—Aug. 19 1670) in their hands, a voluntary captive: and a letter to his parents, which the new convert composed or subscribed (April 15 1670), is darkly tinged with the spirit of popery. But Nature had designed him to think as he pleased, and to speak as he thought: his piety was offended by the excessive worship of creatures; and the study of physics convinced him of the impossibility of transubstantiation, which is abundantly refuted by the testimony of our senses. His return to the communion of a falling sect was a bold and disinterested step, that exposed him to the rigour of the laws; and a speedy flight to Geneva protected him from the resentment of his spiritual tyrants, unconscious as they were of the full value of the prize, which they had lost. Had Bayle adhered to the catholic church, had he embraced the ecclesiastical profession, the genius and favour of such a proselyte might have aspired to wealth and honours in his native country: but the hypocrite would have found less happiness in the comforts of a benefice, or the dignity of a mitre, than he enjoyed at Rotterdam in a private state of exile, indigence, and freedom. Without a country, or a patron, or a prejudice, he claimed the liberty and subsisted by the labours of his pen: the inequality of his voluminous works is explained and excused by his alternately writing for himself, for the booksellers, and for posterity; and if a severe critic would reduce him to a single folio, that relic, like the books of the Sibyl, would become still more valuable. A calm and lofty spectator of the religious tempest, the philosopher of Rotterdam condemned with equal firmness the persecution of Lewis the Fourteenth, and the republican maxims of the Calvinists; their vain prophecies, and the intolerant bigotry which sometimes vexed his solitary retreat. In reviewing the controversies of the times, he turned against each other the arguments of the disputants; successively wielding the arms of the catholics and protestants, he proves that neither the way of authority, nor the way of examination can afford the multitude any test of religious truth; and dexterously concludes that custom and education must be the sole grounds of popular belief. The ancient paradox of Plutarch, that atheism is less pernicious than superstition, acquires a tenfold vigor, when it is adorned with the colours of his wit, and pointed with the acuteness of his logic. His critical dictionary is a vast repository of facts and opinions; and he balances the false religions in his sceptical scales, till the opposite quantities (if I may use the language of algebra) annihilate each other. The wonderful power which he so boldly exercised, of assembling doubts and objections, had tempted him jocosely to assume the title of the {Greek expression} Zeus, the cloud-compelling Jove; and in a conversation with the ingenious Abbe (afterwards Cardinal) de Polignac, he freely disclosed his universal Pyrrhonism. "I am most truly (said Bayle) a protestant; for I protest indifferently against all systems and all sects."

The academical resentment, which I may possibly have provoked, will prudently spare this plain narrative of my studies, or rather of my idleness; and of the unfortunate event which shortened the term of my residence at Oxford. But it may be suggested, that my father was unlucky in the choice of a society, and the chance of a tutor. It will perhaps be asserted, that in the lapse of forty years many improvements have taken place in the college and in the university. I am not unwilling to believe, that some tutors might have been found more active than Dr. Waldgrave, and less contemptible than Dr.****. About the same time, and in the same walk, a Bentham was still treading in the footsteps of a Burton, whose maxims he had adopted, and whose life he had published. The biographer indeed preferred the school-logic to the new philosophy, Burgursdicius to Locke; and the hero appears, in his own writings, a stiff and conceited pedant. Yet even these men, according to the measure of their capacity, might be diligent and useful; and it is recorded of Burton, that he taught his pupils what he knew; some Latin, some Greek, some ethics and metaphysics; referring them to proper masters for the languages and sciences of which he was ignorant. At a more recent period, many students have been attracted by the merit and reputation of Sir William Scott, then a tutor in University College, and now conspicuous in the profession of the civil law: my personal acquaintance with that gentleman has inspired me with a just esteem for his abilities and knowledge; and I am assured that his lectures on history would compose, were they given to the public, a most valuable treatise. Under the auspices of the present Archbishop of York, Dr. Markham, himself an eminent scholar, a more regular discipline has been introduced, as I am told, at Christ Church; a course of classical and philosophical studies is proposed, and even pursued, in that numerous seminary: learning has been made a duty, a pleasure, and even a fashion; and several young gentlemen do honour to the college in which they have been educated. According to the will of the donor, the profit of the second part of Lord Clarendon's History has been applied to the establishment of a riding-school, that the polite exercises might be taught, I know not with what success, in the university. The Vinerian professorship is of far more serious importance; the laws of his country are the first science of an Englishman of rank and fortune, who is called to be a magistrate, and may hope to be a legislator. This judicious institution was coldly entertained by the graver doctors, who complained (I have heard the complaint) that it would take the young people from their books: but Mr. Viner's benefaction is not unprofitable, since it has at least produced the excellent commentaries of Sir William Blackstone.

After carrying me to Putney, to the house of his friend Mr. Mallet, by whose philosophy I was rather scandalized than reclaimed, it was necessary for my father to form a new plan of education, and to devise some method which, if possible, might effect the cure of my spiritual malady. After much debate it was determined, from the advice and personal experience of Mr. Eliot (now Lord Eliot) to fix me, during some years, at Lausanne in Switzerland. Mr. Frey, a Swiss gentleman of Basil, undertook the conduct of the journey: we left London the 19th of June, crossed the sea from Dover to Calais, travelled post through several provinces of France, by the direct road of St. Quentin, Rheims, Langres, and Besancon, and arrived the 30th of June at Lausanne, where I was immediately settled under the roof and tuition of Mr. Pavilliard, a Calvinist minister.

The first marks of my father's displeasure rather astonished than afflicted me: when he threatened to banish, and disown, and disinherit a rebellious son, I cherished a secret hope that he would not be able or willing to effect his menaces; and the pride of conscience encouraged me to sustain the honourable and important part which I was now acting. My spirits were raised and kept alive by the rapid motion of my journey, the new and various scenes of the Continent, and the civility of Mr. Frey, a man of sense, who was not ignorant of books or the world. But after he had resigned me into Pavilliard's hands, and I was fixed in my new habitation, I had leisure to contemplate the strange and melancholy prospect before me. My first complaint arose from my ignorance of the language. In my childhood I had once studied the French grammar, and I could imperfectly understand the easy prose of a familiar subject. But when I was thus suddenly cast on a foreign land, I found myself deprived of the use of speech and of hearing; and, during some weeks, incapable not only of enjoying the pleasures of conversation, but even of asking or answering a question in the common intercourse of life. To a home-bred Englishman every object, every custom was offensive; but the native of any country might have been disgusted with the general aspect of his lodging and entertainment. I had now exchanged my elegant apartment in Magdalen College, for a narrow, gloomy street, the most unfrequented of an unhandsome town, for an old inconvenient house, and for a small chamber ill-contrived and ill-furnished, which, on the approach of Winter, instead of a companionable fire, must be warmed by the dull invisible heat of a stove. From a man I was again degraded to the dependence of a schoolboy. Mr. Pavilliard managed my expences, which had been reduced to a diminutive state: I received a small monthly allowance for my pocket-money; and helpless and awkward as I have ever been, I no longer enjoyed the indispensable comfort of a servant. My condition seemed as destitute of hope, as it was devoid of pleasure: I was separated for an indefinite, which appeared an infinite term from my native country; and I had lost all connexion with my catholic friends. I have since reflected with surprise, that as the Romish clergy of every part of Europe maintain a close correspondence with each other, they never attempted, by letters or messages, to rescue me from the hands of the heretics, or at least to confirm my zeal and constancy in the profession of the faith. Such was my first introduction to Lausanne; a place where I spent nearly five years with pleasure and profit, which I afterwards revisited without compulsion, and which I have finally selected as the most grateful retreat for the decline of my life.

But it is the peculiar felicity of youth that the most unpleasing objects and events seldom make a deep or lasting impression; it forgets the past, enjoys the present, and anticipates the future. At the flexible age of sixteen I soon learned to endure, and gradually to adopt, the new forms of arbitrary manners: the real hardships of my situation were alienated by time. Had I been sent abroad in a more splendid style, such as the fortune and bounty of my father might have supplied, I might have returned home with the same stock of language and science, which our countrymen usually import from the Continent. An exile and a prisoner as I was, their example betrayed me into some irregularities of wine, of play, and of idle excursions: but I soon felt the impossibility of associating with them on equal terms; and after the departure of my first acquaintance, I held a cold and civil correspondence with their successors. This seclusion from English society was attended with the most solid benefits. In the Pays de Vaud, the French language is used with less imperfection than in most of the distant provinces of France: in Pavilliard's family, necessity compelled me to listen and to speak; and if I was at first disheartened by the apparent slowness, in a few months I was astonished by the rapidity of my progress. My pronunciation was formed by the constant repetition of the same sounds; the variety of words and idioms, the rules of grammar, and distinctions of genders, were impressed in my memory ease and freedom were obtained by practice; correctness and elegance by labour; and before I was recalled home, French, in which I spontaneously thought, was more familiar than English to my ear, my tongue, and my pen. The first effect of this opening knowledge was the revival of my love of reading, which had been chilled at Oxford; and I soon turned over, without much choice, almost all the French books in my tutor's library. Even these amusements were productive of real advantage: my taste and judgment were now somewhat riper. I was introduced to a new mode of style and literature: by the comparison of manners and opinions, my views were enlarged, my prejudices were corrected, and a copious voluntary abstract of the Histoire de l'Eglise et de l'Empire, by le Sueur, may be placed in a middle line between my childish and my manly studies. As soon as I was able to converse with the natives, I began to feel some satisfaction in their company my awkward timidity was polished and emboldened; and I frequented, for the first time, assemblies of men and women. The acquaintance of the Pavilliards prepared me by degrees for more elegant society. I was received with kindness and indulgence in the best families of Lausanne; and it was in one of these that I formed an intimate and lasting connection with Mr. Deyverdun, a young man of an amiable temper and excellent understanding. In the arts of fencing and dancing, small indeed was my proficiency; and some months were idly wasted in the riding-school. My unfitness to bodily exercise reconciled me to a sedentary life, and the horse, the favourite of my countrymen, never contributed to the pleasures of my youth.

My obligations to the lessons of Mr. Pavilliard, gratitude will not suffer me to forget: he was endowed with a clear head and a warm heart; his innate benevolence had assuaged the spirit of the church; he was rational, because he was moderate: in the course of his studies he had acquired a just though superficial knowledge of most branches of literature; by long practice, he was skilled in the arts of teaching; and he laboured with assiduous patience to know the character, gain the affection, and open the mind of his English pupil. As soon as we began to understand each other, he gently led me, from a blind and undistinguishing love of reading, into the path of instruction. I consented with pleasure that a portion of the morning hours should be consecrated to a plan of modern history and geography, and to the critical perusal of the French and Latin classics; and at each step I felt myself invigorated by the habits of application and method. His prudence repressed and dissembled some youthful sallies; and as soon as I was confirmed in the habits of industry and temperance, he gave the reins into my own hands. His favourable report of my behaviour and progress gradually obtained some latitude of action and expence; and he wished to alleviate the hardships of my lodging and entertainment. The principles of philosophy were associated with the examples of taste; and by a singular chance, the book, as well as the man, which contributed the most effectually to my education, has a stronger claim on my gratitude than on my admiration. Mr. De Crousaz, the adversary of Bayle and Pope, is not distinguished by lively fancy or profound reflection; and even in his own country, at the end of a few years, his name and writings are almost obliterated. But his philosophy had been formed in the school of Locke, his divinity in that of Limborch and Le Clerc; in a long and laborious life, several generations of pupils were taught to think, and even to write; his lessons rescued the academy of Lausanne from Calvinistic prejudice; and he had the rare merit of diffusing a more liberal spirit among the clergy and people of the Pays de Vaud. His system of logic, which in the last editions has swelled to six tedious and prolix volumes, may be praised as a clear and methodical abridgment of the art of reasoning, from our simple ideas to the most complex operations of the human understanding. This system I studied, and meditated, and abstracted, till I have obtained the free command of an universal instrument, which I soon presumed to exercise on my catholic opinions. Pavilliard was not unmindful that his first task, his most important duty, was to reclaim me from the errors of popery. The intermixture of sects has rendered the Swiss clergy acute and learned on the topics of controversy; and I have some of his letters in which he celebrates the dexterity of his attack, and my gradual concessions after a firm and well-managed defence. I was willing, and I am now willing, to allow him a handsome share of the honour of my conversion: yet I must observe, that it was principally effected by my private reflections; and I still remember my solitary transport at the discovery of a philosophical argument against the doctrine of transubstantiation: that the text of scripture, which seems to inculcate the real presence, is attested only by a single sense—our sight; while the real presence itself is disproved by three of our senses—the sight, the touch, and the taste. The various articles of the Romish creed disappeared like a dream; and after a full conviction, on Christmas-day, 1754, I received the sacrament in the church of Lausanne. It was here that I suspended my religious inquiries, acquiescing with implicit belief in the tenets and mysteries, which are adopted by the general consent of catholics and protestants.

Such, from my arrival at Lausanne, during the first eighteen or twenty months (July 1753—March 1755), were my useful studies, the foundation of all my future improvements. But every man who rises above the common level has received two educations: the first from his teachers; the second, more personal and important, from himself. He will not, like the fanatics of the last age, define the moment of grace; but he cannot forget the aera of his life, in which his mind has expanded to its proper form and dimensions. My worthy tutor had the good sense and modesty to discern how far he could be useful: as soon as he felt that I advanced beyond his speed and measure, he wisely left me to my genius; and the hours of lesson were soon lost in the voluntary labour of the whole morning, and sometimes of the whole day. The desire of prolonging my time, gradually confirmed the salutary habit of early rising, to which I have always adhered, with some regard to seasons and situations; but it is happy for my eyes and my health, that my temperate ardour has never been seduced to trespass on the hours of the night. During the last three years of my residence at Lausanne, I may assume the merit of serious and solid application; but I am tempted to distinguish the last eight months of the year 1755, as the period of the most extraordinary diligence and rapid progress. In my French and Latin translations I adopted an excellent method, which, from my own success, I would recommend to the imitation of students. I chose some classic writer, such as Cicero and Vertot, the most approved for purity and elegance of style. I translated, for instance, an epistle of Cicero into French; and after throwing it aside, till the words and phrases were obliterated from my memory, I re-translated my French into such Latin as I could find; and then compared each sentence of my imperfect version, with the ease, the grace, the propriety of the Roman orator. A similar experiment was made on several pages of the Revolutions of Vertot; I turned them into Latin, returned them after a sufficient interval into my own French, and again scrutinized the resemblance or dissimilitude of the copy and the original. By degrees I was less ashamed, by degrees I was more satisfied with myself; and I persevered in the practice of these double translations, which filled several books, till I had acquired the knowledge or both idioms, and the command at least of a correct style. This useful exercise of writing was accompanied and succeeded by the more pleasing occupation of reading the best authors. The perusal of the Roman classics was at once my exercise and reward. Dr. Middleton's History, which I then appreciated above its true value, naturally directed the to the writings of Cicero. The most perfect editions, that of Olivet, which may adorn the shelves of the rich, that of Ernesti, which should lie on the table of the learned, were not in my power. For the familiar epistles I used the text and English commentary of Bishop Ross: but my general edition was that of Verburgius, published at Amsterdam in two large volumes in folio, with an indifferent choice of various notes. I read, with application and pleasure, all the epistles, all the orations, and the most important treatises of rhetoric and philosophy; and as I read, I applauded the observation of Quintilian, that every student may judge of his own proficiency, by the satisfaction which he receives from the Roman orator. I tasted the beauties of language, I breathed the spirit of freedom, and I imbibed from his precepts and examples the public and private sense of a man. Cicero in Latin, and Xenophon in Greek, are indeed the two ancients whom I would first propose to a liberal scholar; not only for the merit of their style and sentiments, but for the admirable lessons, which may be applied almost to every situation of public and private life. Cicero's Epistles may in particular afford the models of every form of correspondence, from the careless effusions of tenderness and friendship, to the well guarded declaration of discreet and dignified resentment. After finishing this great author, a library of eloquence and reason, I formed a more extensive plan of reviewing the Latin classics, under the four divisions of, 1. historians, 2. Poets, 3. orators, and 4. philosophers, in a chronological series, from the days of Plautus and Sallust, to the decline of the language and empire of Rome: and this plan, in the last twenty-seven months of my residence at Lausanne (Jan. 1756—April 1758), I nearly accomplished. Nor was this review, however rapid, either hasty or superficial. I indulged myself in a second and even a third perusal of Terence, Virgil, Horace, Tacitus, &c.; and studied to imbibe the sense and spirit most congenial to my own. I never suffered a difficult or corrupt passage to escape, till I had viewed it in every light of which it was susceptible: though often disappointed, I always consulted the most learned or ingenious commentators, Torrentius and Dacier on Horace, Catrou and Servius on Virgil, Lipsius on Tacitus, Meziriac on Ovid, &c.; and in the ardour of my inquiries, I embraced a large circle of historical and critical erudition. My abstracts of each book were made in the French language: my observations often branched into particular essays; and I can still read, without contempt, a dissertation of eight folio pages on eight lines (287-294) of the fourth Georgic of Virgil. Mr. Deyverdun, my friend, whose name will be frequently repeated, had joined with equal zeal, though not with equal perseverance, in the same undertaking. To him every thought, every composition, was instantly communicated; with him

I enjoyed the benefits of a free conversation on the topics of our common studies.

But it is scarcely possible for a mind endowed with any active curiosity to be long conversant with the Latin classics, without aspiring to know the Greek originals, whom they celebrate as their masters, and of whom they so warmly recommend the study and imitation;

—Vos exemplaria Graeca
Nocturna versate manu, versate diurna.

It was now that I regretted the early years which had been wasted in sickness or idleness, or mere idle reading; that I condemned the perverse method of our schoolmasters, who, by first teaching the mother-language, might descend with so much ease and perspicuity to the origin and etymology of a derivative idiom. In the nineteenth year of my age I determined to supply this defect; and the lessons of Pavilliard again contributed to smooth the entrance of the way, the Greek alphabet, the grammar, and the pronunciation according to the French accent. At my earnest request we presumed to open the Iliad; and I had the pleasure of beholding, though darkly and through a glass, the true image of Homer, whom I had long since admired in an English dress. After my tutor had left me to myself, I worked my way through about half the Iliad, and afterwards interpreted alone a large portion of Xenophon and Herodotus. But my ardour, destitute of aid and emulation, was gradually cooled, and, from the barren task of searching words in a lexicon, I withdrew to the free and familiar conversation of Virgil and Tacitus. Yet in my residence at Lausanne I had laid a solid foundation, which enabled me, in a more propitious season, to prosecute the study of Grecian literature.

From a blind idea of the usefulness of such abstract science, my father had been desirous, and even pressing, that I should devote some time to the mathematics; nor could I refuse to comply with so reasonable a wish. During two winters I attended the private lectures of Monsieur de Traytorrens, who explained the elements of algebra and geometry, as far as the conic sections of the Marquis de l'Hopital, and appeared satisfied with my diligence and improvement. But as my childish propensity for numbers and calculations was totally extinct, I was content to receive the passive impression of my Professor's lectures, without any active exercise of my own powers. As soon as I understood the principles, I relinquished for ever the pursuit of the mathematics; nor can I lament that I desisted, before my mind was hardened by the habit of rigid demonstration, so destructive of the finer feelings of moral evidence, which must, however, determine the actions and opinions of our lives. I listened with more pleasure to the proposal of studying the law of nature and nations, which was taught in the academy of Lausanne by Mr. Vicat, a professor of some learning and reputation. But instead of attending his public or private course, I preferred in my closet the lessons of his masters, and my own reason. Without being disgusted by Grotius or Puffendorf, I studied in their writings the duties of a man, the rights of a citizen, the theory of justice (it is, alas! a theory), and the laws of peace and war, which have had some influence on the practice of modern Europe. My fatigues were alleviated by the good sense of their commentator Barbeyrac. Locke's Treatise of Government instructed me in the knowledge of Whig principles, which are rather founded in reason than experience; but my delight was in the frequent perusal of Montesquieu, whose energy of style, and boldness of hypothesis, were powerful to awaken and stimulate the genius of the age. The logic of De Crousaz had prepared me to engage with his master Locke and his antagonist Bayle; of whom the former may be used as a bridle, and the latter applied as a spur, to the curiosity of a young philosopher. According to the nature of their respective works, the schools of argument and objection, I carefully went through the Essay on Human Understanding, and occasionally consulted the most interesting articles of the Philosophic Dictionary. In the infancy of my reason I turned over, as an idle amusement, the most serious and important treatise: in its maturity, the most trifling performance could exercise my taste or judgment, and more than once I have been led by a novel into a deep and instructive train of thinking. But I cannot forbear to mention three particular books, since they may have remotely contributed to form the historian of the Roman empire. 1. From the Provincial Letters of Pascal, which almost every year I have perused with new pleasure, I learned to manage the weapon of grave and temperate irony, even on subjects of ecclesiastical solemnity. 2. The Life of

Julian, by the Abbe de la Bleterie, first introduced me to the man and the times; and I should be glad to recover my first essay on the truth of the miracle which stopped the rebuilding of the Temple of Jerusalem. 3. In Giannone's Civil History of Naples I observed with a critical eye the progress and abuse of sacerdotal power, and the revolutions of Italy in the darker ages. This various reading, which I now conducted with discretion, was digested, according to the precept and model of Mr. Locke, into a large common-place book; a practice, however, which I do not strenuously recommend. The action of the pen will doubtless imprint an idea on the mind as well as on the paper: but I much question whether the benefits of this laborious method are adequate to the waste of time; and I must agree with Dr. Johnson, (Idler, No. 74.) "that what is twice read, is commonly better remembered, than what is transcribed."

During two years, if I forget some boyish excursions of a day or a week, I was fixed at Lausanne; but at the end of the third summer, my father consented that I should make the tour of Switzerland with Pavilliard: and our short absence of one month (Sept. 21st—Oct. 20th, 1755) was a reward and relaxation of my assiduous studies. The fashion of climbing the mountains and reviewing the Glaciers, had not yet been introduced by foreign travellers, who seek the sublime beauties of nature. But the political face of the country is not less diversified by the forms and spirit of so many various republics, from the jealous government of the few to the licentious freedom of the many. I contemplated with pleasure the new prospects of men and manners; though my conversation with the natives would have been more free and instructive, had I possessed the German, as well as the French language. We passed through most of the principal towns of Switzerland; Neufchatel, Bienne, Soleurre, Arau, Baden, Zurich, Basil, and Berne. In every place we visited the churches, arsenals, libraries, and all the most eminent persons; and after my return, I digested my notes in fourteen or fifteen sheets of a French journal, which I dispatched to my father, as a proof that my time and his money had not been mis-spent. Had I found this journal among his papers, I might be tempted to select some passages; but I will not transcribe the printed accounts, and it may be sufficient to notice a remarkable spot, which left a deep and lasting impression on my memory. From Zurich we proceeded to the Benedictine Abbey of Einfidlen, snore commonly styled Our

Lady of the Hermits. I was astonished by the profuse ostentation of riches in the poorest corner of Europe; amidst a savage scene of woods and mountains, a palace appears to have been erected by magic; and it was erected by the potent magic of religion. A crowd of palmers and votaries was prostrate before the altar. The title and worship of the Mother of God provoked my indignation; and the lively naked image of superstition suggested to me, as in the same place it had done to Zuinglius, the most pressing argument for the reformation of the church. About two years after this tour, I passed at Geneva a useful and agreeable month; but this excursion, and short visits in the Pays de Vaud, did not materially interrupt my studious and sedentary life at Lausanne.

My thirst of improvement, and the languid state of science at Lausanne, soon prompted me to solicit a literary correspondence with several men of learning, whom I had not an opportunity of personally consulting. 1. In the perusal of Livy, (xxx. 44,) I had been stopped by a sentence in a speech of Hannibal, which cannot be reconciled by any torture with his character or argument. The commentators dissemble, or confess their perplexity. It occurred to me, that the change of a single letter, by substituting otio instead of odio, might restore a clear and consistent sense; but I wished to weigh my emendation in scales less partial than my own. I addressed myself to M. Crevier, the successor of Rollin, and a professor in the university of Paris, who had published a large and valuable edition of Livy. His answer was speedy and polite; he praised my ingenuity, and adopted my conjecture. 2. I maintained a Latin correspondence, at first anonymous, and afterwards in my own name, with Professor Breitinger of Zurich, the learned editor of a Septuagint Bible. In our frequent letters we discussed many questions of antiquity, many passages of the Latin classics. I proposed my interpretations and amendments. His censures, for he did not spare my boldness of conjecture, were sharp and strong; and I was encouraged by the consciousness of my strength, when I could stand in free debate against a critic of such eminence and erudition. 3. I corresponded on similar topics with the celebrated Professor Matthew Gesner, of the university of Gottingen; and he accepted, as courteously as the two former, the invitation of an unknown youth. But his abilities might possibly be decayed; his elaborate letters were feeble and prolix; and when

I asked his proper direction, the vain old man covered half a sheet of paper with the foolish enumeration of his titles and offices. 4. These Professors of Paris, Zurich, and Gottingen, were strangers, whom I presumed to address on the credit of their name; but Mr. Allamand, Minister at Bex, was my personal friend, with whom I maintained a more free and interesting correspondence. He was a master of language, of science, and, above all, of dispute; and his acute and flexible logic could support, with equal address, and perhaps with equal indifference, the adverse sides of every possible question. His spirit was active, but his pen had been indolent. Mr. Allamand had exposed himself to much scandal and reproach, by an anonymous letter (1745) to the Protestants of France; in which he labours to persuade them that public worship is the exclusive right and duty of the state, and that their numerous assemblies of dissenters and rebels were not authorized by the law or the gospel. His style is animated, his arguments specious; and if the papist may seem to lurk under the mask of a protestant, the philosopher is concealed under the disguise of a papist. After some trials in France and Holland, which were defeated by his fortune or his character, a genius that might have enlightened or deluded the world, was buried in a country living, unknown to fame, and discontented with mankind. Est sacrificulus in pago, et rusticos decipit. As often as private or ecclesiastical business called him to Lausanne, I enjoyed the pleasure and benefit of his conversation, and we were mutually flattered by our attention to each other. Our correspondence, in his absence, chiefly turned on Locke's metaphysics, which he attacked, and I defended; the origin of ideas, the principles of evidence, and the doctrine of liberty;

And found no end, in wandering mazes lost.

By fencing with so skilful a master, I acquired some dexterity in the use of my philosophic weapons; but I was still the slave of education and prejudice. He had some measures to keep; and I much suspect that he never showed me the true colours of his secret scepticism.

Before I was recalled from Switzerland, I had the satisfaction of seeing the most extraordinary man of the age; a poet, an historian, a philosopher, who has filled thirty quartos, of prose and verse, with his various productions, often excellent, and always entertaining. Need I add the name of Voltaire? After forfeiting, by his own misconduct, the friendship of the first of kings, he retired, at the age of sixty, with a plentiful fortune, to a free and beautiful country, and resided two winters (1757 and 1758) in the town or neighbourhood of Lausanne. My desire of beholding Voltaire, whom I then rated above his real magnitude, was easily gratified. He received me with civility as an English youth; but I cannot boast of any peculiar notice or distinction, Virgilium vidi tantum.

The ode which he composed on his first arrival on the banks of the Leman Lake, O Maison d'Aristippe! O Jardin d'Epicure, &c. had been imparted as a secret to the gentleman by whom I was introduced. He allowed me to read it twice; I knew it by heart; and as my discretion was not equal to my memory, the author was soon displeased by the circulation of a copy. In writing this trivial anecdote, I wished to observe whether my memory was impaired, and I have the comfort of finding that every line of the poem is still engraved in fresh and indelible characters. The highest gratification which I derived from Voltaire's residence at Lausanne, was the uncommon circumstance of hearing a great poet declaim his own productions on the stage. He had formed a company of gentlemen and ladies, some of whom were not destitute of talents. A decent theatre was framed at Monrepos, a country-house at the end of a suburb; dresses and scenes were provided at the expense of the actors; and the author directed the rehearsals with the zeal and attention of paternal love. In two successive winters his tragedies of Zayre, Alzire, Zulime, and his sentimental comedy of the Enfant Prodigue, were played at the theatre of Monrepos. Voltaire represented the characters best adapted to his years, Lusignan, Alvarez, Benassar, Euphemon. His declamation was fashioned to the pomp and cadence of the old stage; and he expressed the enthusiasm of poetry, rather than the feelings of nature. My ardour, which soon became conspicuous, seldom failed of procuring me a ticket. The habits of pleasure fortified my taste for the French theatre, and that taste has perhaps abated my idolatry for the gigantic genius of Shakespeare, which is inculcated from our infancy as the first duty of an Englishman. The wit and philosophy of Voltaire, his table and theatre, refined, in a visible degree, the manners of Lausanne; and, however addicted to study, I enjoyed my share of the amusements of society. After the representation of Monrepos I sometimes supped with the actors. I was now familiar in some, and acquainted in many houses; and my evenings were generally devoted to cards and conversation, either in private parties or numerous assemblies.

I hesitate, from the apprehension of ridicule, when I approach the delicate subject of my early love. By this word I do not mean the polite attention, the gallantry, without hope or design, which has originated in the spirit of chivalry, and is interwoven with the texture of French manners. I understand by this passion the union of desire, friendship, and tenderness, which is inflamed by a single female, which prefers her to the rest of her sex, and which seeks her possession as the supreme or the sole happiness of our being. I need not blush at recollecting the object of my choice; and though my love was disappointed of success, I am rather proud that I was once capable of feeling such a pure and exalted sentiment. The personal attractions of Mademoiselle Susan Curchod were embellished by the virtues and talents of the mind. Her fortune was humble, but her family was respectable. Her mother, a native of France, had preferred her religion to her country. The profession of her father did not extinguish the moderation and philosophy of his temper, and he lived content with a small salary and laborious duty, in the obscure lot of minister of Crassy, in the mountains that separate the Pays de Vaud from the county of Burgundy. In the solitude of a sequestered village he bestowed a liberal, and even learned, education on his only daughter. She surpassed his hopes by her proficiency in the sciences and languages; and in her short visits to some relations at Lausanne, the wit, the beauty, and erudition of Mademoiselle Curchod were the theme of universal applause. The report of such a prodigy awakened my curiosity; I saw and loved. I found her learned without pedantry, lively in conversation, pure in sentiment, and elegant in manners; and the first sudden emotion was fortified by the habits and knowledge of a more familiar acquaintance. She permitted me to make her two or three visits at her father's house. I passed some happy days there, in the mountains of Burgundy, and her parents honourably encouraged the connection. In a calm retirement the gay vanity of youth no longer fluttered in her bosom; she listened to the voice of truth and passion, and I might presume to hope that I had made some impression on a virtuous heart. At Crassy and Lausanne I indulged my dream of felicity: but on my return to England, I soon discovered that my father would not hear of this strange alliance, and that without his consent I was myself destitute and helpless. After a painful struggle I yielded to my fate: I sighed as a lover, I obeyed as a son; my wound was insensibly healed by time, absence, and the habits of a new life. My cure was accelerated by a faithful report of the tranquillity and cheerfulness of the lady herself, and my love subsided in friendship and esteem. The minister of Crassy soon afterwards died; his stipend died with him: his daughter retired to Geneva, where, by teaching young ladies, she earned a hard subsistence for herself and her mother; but in her lowest distress she maintained a spotless reputation, and a dignified behaviour. A rich banker of Paris, a citizen of Geneva, had the good fortune and good sense to discover and possess this inestimable treasure; and in the capital of taste and luxury she resisted the temptations of wealth, as she had sustained the hardships of indigence. The genius of her husband has exalted him to the most conspicuous station in Europe. In every change of prosperity and disgrace he has reclined on the bosom of a faithful friend; and Mademoiselle Curchod is now the wife of M. Necker, the minister, and perhaps the legislator, of the French monarchy.

Whatsoever have been the fruits of my education, they must be ascribed to the fortunate banishment which placed me at Lausanne. I have sometimes applied to my own fate the verses of Pindar, which remind an Olympic champion that his victory was the consequence of his exile; and that at home, like a domestic fowl, his days might have rolled away inactive or inglorious.

[Greek omitted]

> Thus, like the crested bird of Mars, at home
>   Engag'd in foul domestic jars,
>   And wasted with intestine wars,
> Inglorious hadst thou spent thy vig'rous bloom;
>   Had not sedition's civil broils
>   Expell'd thee from thy native Crete,
>   And driv'n thee with more glorious toils
> Th' Olympic crown in Pisa's plain to meet.
>   West's Pindar.

If my childish revolt against the religion of my country had not stripped me in time of my academic gown, the five important years, so liberally improved in the studies and conversation of Lausanne, would have been steeped in port and prejudice among the monks of Oxford. Had the fatigue of idleness compelled me to read, the path of learning would not have been enlightened by a ray of philosophic freedom. I should have grown to manhood ignorant of the life and language of Europe, and my knowledge of the world would have been confined to an English cloister. But my religious error fixed me at Lausanne, in a state of banishment and disgrace. The rigid course of discipline and abstinence, to which I was condemned, invigorated the constitution of my mind and body; poverty and pride estranged me from my countrymen. One mischief, however, and in their eyes a serious and irreparable mischief, was derived from the success of my Swiss education; I had ceased to be an Englishman. At the flexible period of youth, from the age of sixteen to twenty-one, my opinions, habits, and sentiments were cast in a foreign mould; the faint and distant remembrance of England was almost obliterated; my native language was grown less familiar; and I should have cheerfully accepted the offer of a moderate independence on the terms of perpetual exile. By the good sense and temper of Pavilliard my yoke was insensibly lightened: he left me master of my time and actions; but he could neither change my situation, nor increase my allowance, and with the progress of my years and reason I impatiently sighed for the moment of my deliverance. At length, in the spring of the year 1758, my father signified his permission and his pleasure that I should immediately return home. We were then in the midst of a war: the resentment of the French at our taking their ships without a declaration, had rendered that polite nation somewhat peevish and difficult. They denied a passage to English travellers, and the road through Germany was circuitous, toilsome, and perhaps in the neighbourhood of the armies, exposed to some danger. In this perplexity, two Swiss officers of my acquaintance in the Dutch service, who were returning to their garrisons, offered to conduct me through France as one of their companions; nor did we sufficiently reflect that my borrowed name and regimentals might have been considered, in case of a discovery, in a very serious light. I took my leave of Lausanne on April 11 1758, with a mixture of joy and regret, in the firm resolution revisiting, as a man, the persons and places which had been so dear to my youth. We travelled slowly, but pleasantly, in a hired coach, over the hills of Franche-compte and the fertile province of Lorraine, and passed, without accident or inquiry, through several fortified towns of the French frontier: from thence we entered the wild Ardennes of the Austrian dutchy of Luxemburg; and after crossing the Meuse at Liege, we traversed the heaths of Brabant, and reached, on April 26, our Dutch garrison of Bois le Duc. In our passage through Nancy, my eye was gratified by the aspect of a regular and beautiful city, the work of Stanislaus, who, after the storms of Polish royalty, reposed in the love and gratitude of his new subjects of Lorraine. In our halt at Maestricht I visited Mr. de Beaufort, a learned critic, who was known to me by his specious arguments against the five first centuries of the Roman History. After dropping my regimental companions, I stepped aside to visit Rotterdam and the Hague. I wished to have observed a country, the monument of freedom and industry; but my days were numbered, and a longer delay would have been ungraceful. I hastened to embark at the Brill, landed the next day at Harwich, and proceeded to London, where my father awaited my arrival. The whole term of my first absence from England was four years ten months and fifteen days.

In the prayers of the church our personal concerns are judiciously reduced to the threefold distinction of mind, body, and estate. The sentiments of the mind excite and exercise our social sympathy. The review of my moral and literary character is the most interesting to myself and to the public; and I may expatiate, without reproach, on my private studies; since they have produced the public writings, which can alone entitle me to the esteem and friendship of my readers. The experience of the world inculcates a discreet reserve on the subject of our person and estate, and we soon learn that a free disclosure of our riches or poverty would provoke the malice of envy, or encourage the insolence of contempt.

The only person in England whom I was impatient to see was my aunt Porten, the affectionate guardian of my tender years. I hastened to her house in College-street, Westminster; and the evening was spent in the effusions of joy and confidence. It was not without some awe and apprehension that I approached the presence of my father. My infancy, to speak the truth, had been neglected at home; the severity of his look and language at our last parting still dwelt on my memory; nor could I form any notion of his character, or my probable reception. They were both more agreeable than I could expect. The domestic discipline of our ancestors has been relaxed by the philosophy and softness of the age; and if my father remembered that he had trembled before a stern parent, it was only to adopt with his own son an opposite mode of behaviour. He received me as a man and a friend; all constraint was banished at our first interview, and we ever afterwards continued on the same terms of easy and equal politeness. He applauded the success of my education; every word and action was expressive of the most cordial affection; and our lives would have passed without a cloud, if his oeconomy had been equal to his fortune, or if his fortune had been equal to his desires. During my absence he had married his second wife, Miss Dorothea Patton, who was introduced to me with the most unfavourable prejudice. I considered his second marriage as an act of displeasure, and I was disposed to hate the rival of my mother. But the injustice was in my own fancy, and the imaginary monster was an amiable and deserving woman. I could not be mistaken in the first view of her understanding, her knowledge, and the elegant spirit of her conversation: her polite welcome, and her assiduous care to study and gratify my wishes, announced at least that the surface would be smooth; and my suspicions of art and falsehood were gradually dispelled by the full discovery of her warm and exquisite sensibility. After some reserve on my side, our minds associated in confidence and friendship; and as Mrs. Gibbon had neither children nor the hopes of children, we more easily adopted the tender names and genuine characters of mother and of son. By the indulgence of these parents, I was left at liberty to consult my taste or reason in the choice of place, of company, and of amusements; and my excursions were bounded only by the limits of the island, and the measure of my income. Some faint efforts were made to procure me the employment of secretary to a foreign embassy; and I listened to a scheme which would again have transported me to the continent. Mrs. Gibbon, with seeming wisdom, exhorted me to take chambers in the Temple, and devote my leisure to the study of the law. I cannot repent of having neglected her advice. Few men, without the spur of necessity, have resolution to force their way, through the thorns and thickets of that gloomy labyrinth. Nature had not endowed me with the bold and ready eloquence which makes itself heard amidst the tumult of the bar; and I should probably have been diverted from the labours of literature, without acquiring the fame or fortune of a successful pleader. I had no need to call to my aid the regular duties of a profession; every day, every hour, was agreeably filled; nor have I known, like so many of my countrymen, the tediousness of an idle life.

Of the two years (May 1758-May 1760,) between my return to England and the embodying of the Hampshire militia, I passed about nine months in London, and the remainder in the country. The metropolis affords many amusements, which are open to all. It is itself an astonishing and perpetual spectacle to the curious eye; and each taste, each sense may be gratified by the variety of objects which will occur in the long circuit of a morning walk. I assiduously frequented the theatres at a very propitious aera of the stage, when a constellation of excellent actors, both in tragedy and comedy, was eclipsed by the meridian brightness of Garrick in the maturity of his judgment, and vigour of his performance. The pleasures of a town-life are within the reach of every man who is regardless of his health, his money, and his company. By the contagion of example I was sometimes seduced; but the better habits, which I had formed at Lausanne, induced me to seek a more elegant and rational society; and if my search was less easy and successful than I might have hoped, I shall at present impute the failure to the disadvantages of my situation and character. Had the rank and fortune of my parents given them an annual establishment in London, their own house would have introduced me to a numerous and polite circle of acquaintance. But my father's taste had always preferred the highest and the lowest company, for which he was equally qualified; and after a twelve years' retirement, he was no longer in the memory of the great with whom he had associated. I found myself a stranger in the midst of a vast and unknown city; and at my entrance into life I was reduced to some dull family parties, and some scattered connections, which were not such as I should have chosen for myself. The most useful friends of my father were the Mallets: they received me with civility and kindness at first on his account, and afterwards on my own; and (if I may use Lord Chesterfield's words) I was soon domesticated in their house. Mr. Mallet, a name among the English poets, is praised by an unforgiving enemy, for the ease and elegance of his conversation, and his wife was not destitute of wit or learning. By his assistance I was introduced to Lady Hervey, the mother of the present earl of Bristol. Her age and infirmities confined her at home; her dinners were select; in the evening her house was open to the best company of both sexes and all nations; nor was I displeased at her preference and affectation of the manners, the language, and the literature of France. But my progress in the English world was in general left to my own efforts, and those efforts were languid and slow. I had not been endowed by art or nature with those happy gifts of confidence and address, which unlock every door and every bosom; nor would it be reasonable to complain of the just consequences of my sickly childhood, foreign education, and reserved temper. While coaches were rattling through Bond-street, I have passed many a solitary evening in my lodging with my books. My studies were sometimes interrupted by a sigh, which I breathed towards Lausanne; and on the approach of Spring, I withdrew without reluctance from the noisy and extensive scene of crowds without company, and dissipation without pleasure. In each of the twenty-five years of my acquaintance with London (1758-1783) the prospect gradually brightened; and this unfavourable picture most properly belongs to the first period after my return from Switzerland.

My father's residence in Hampshire, where I have passed many light, and some heavy hours, was at Beriton, near Petersfield, one mile from the Portsmouth road, and at the easy distance of fifty-eight miles from London. An old mansion, in a state of decay, had been converted into the fashion and convenience of a modern house: and if strangers had nothing to see, the inhabitants had little to desire. The spot was not happily chosen, at the end of the village and the bottom of the hill: but the aspect of the adjacent grounds was various and cheerful; the downs commanded a noble prospect, and the long hanging woods in sight of the house could not perhaps have been improved by art or expence. My father kept in his own hands the whole of the estate, and even rented some additional land; and whatsoever might be the balance of profit and loss, the farm supplied him with amusement and plenty. The produce maintained a number of men and horses, which were multiplied by the intermixture of domestic and rural servants; and in the intervals of labour the favourite team, a handsome set of bays or greys, was harnessed to the coach. The oeconomy of the house was regulated by the taste and prudence of Mrs. Gibbon. She prided herself in the elegance of her occasional dinners; and from the uncleanly avarice of Madame Pavilliard, I was suddenly transported to the daily neatness and luxury of an English table. Our immediate neighbourhood was rare and rustic; but from the verge of our hills, as far as Chichester and Goodwood, the western district of Sussex was interspersed with noble seats and hospitable families, with whom we cultivated a friendly, and might have enjoyed a very frequent, intercourse. As my stay at Buriton was always voluntary, I was received and dismissed with smiles; but the comforts of my retirement did not depend on the ordinary pleasures of the country. My father could never inspire me with his love and knowledge of farming. I never handled a gun, I seldom mounted an horse; and my philosophic walks were soon terminated by a shady bench, where I was long detained by the sedentary amusement of reading or meditation. At home I occupied a pleasant and spacious apartment; the library on the same floor was soon considered as my peculiar domain; and I might say with truth, that I was never less alone than when by myself. My sole complaint, which I piously suppressed, arose from the kind restraint imposed on the freedom of my time. By the habit of early rising I always secured a sacred portion of the day, and many scattered moments were stolen and employed by my studious industry. But the family hours of breakfast, of dinner, of tea, and of supper, were regular and long: after breakfast Mrs. Gibbon expected my company in her dressing-room; after tea my father claimed my conversation and the perusal of the newspapers; and in the midst of an interesting work I was often called down to receive the visit of some idle neighbours. Their dinners and visits required, in due season, a similar return; and I dreaded the period of the full moon, which was usually reserved for our more distant excursions. I could not refuse attending my father, in the summer of 1759, to the races at Stockbridge, Reading, and Odiam, where he had entered a horse for the hunter's plate; and I was not displeased with the sight of our Olympic games, the beauty of the spot, the fleetness of the horses, and the gay tumult of the numerous spectators. As soon as the militia business was agitated, many days were tediously consumed in meetings of deputylieutenants at Petersfield, Alton, and Winchester. In the close of the same year, 1759, Sir Simeon (then Mr.) Stewart attempted an unsuccessful contest for the county of Southampton, against Mr. Legge, Chancellor of the Exchequer: a well-known contest, in which Lord Bute's influence was first exerted and censured. Our canvas at Portsmouth and Gosport lasted several days; but the interruption of my studies was compensated in some degree by the spectacle of English manners, and the acquisition of some practical knowledge.

If in a more domestic or more dissipated scene my application was somewhat relaxed, the love of knowledge was inflamed and gratified by the command of books; and I compared the poverty of Lausanne with the plenty of London. My father's study at Buriton was stuffed with much trash of the last age, with much high church divinity and politics, which have long since gone to their proper place: yet it contained some valuable editions of the classics and the fathers, the choice, as it should seem, of Mr. Law; and many English publications of the times had been occasionally added. From this slender beginning I have gradually formed a numerous and select library, the foundation of my works, and the best comfort of my life, both at home and abroad. On the receipt of the first quarter, a large share of my allowance was appropriated to my literary wants. I cannot forget the joy with which I exchanged a bank-note of twenty pounds for the twenty volumes of the Memoirs of the Academy of Inscriptions; nor would it have been easy, by any other expenditure of the same sum, to have procured so large and lasting a fund of rational amusement. At a time when I most assiduously frequented this school of ancient literature, I thus expressed my opinion of a learned and various collection, which since the year 1759 has been doubled in magnitude, though not in merit—"Une de ces societes, qui ont mieux immortalise Louis XIV. qu un ambition souvent pernicieuse aux hommes, commengoit deja ces recherches qui reunissent la justesse de l'esprit, l'amenete & l'eruditlon: ou l'on voit iant des decouvertes, et quelquefois, ce qui ne cede qu'a peine aux decouvertes, une ignorance modeste et savante." The review of my library must be reserved for the period of its maturity; but in this place I may allow myself to observe, that I am not conscious of having ever bought a book from a motive of ostentation, that every volume, before it was deposited on the shelf, was either read or sufficiently examined, and that I soon adopted the tolerating maxim of the elder Pliny, "nullum esse librum tam malum ut non ex aliqua parte prodesset." I could not yet find leisure or courage to renew the pursuit of the Greek language, excepting by reading the lessons of the Old and New Testament every Sunday, when I attended the family to church. The series of my Latin authors was less strenuously completed; but the acquisition, by inheritance or purchase, of the best editions of Cicero, Quintilian, Livy, Tacitus, Ovid, &c. afforded a fair prospect, which I seldom neglected. I persevered in the useful method of abstracts and observations; and a single example may suffice, of a note which had almost swelled into a work. The solution of a passage of Livy (xxxviii. 38,) involved me in the dry and dark treatises of Greaves, Arbuthnot, Hooper, Bernard, Eisenschmidt, Gronovius, La Barre, Freret, &c.; and in my French essay (chap. 20,) I ridiculously send the reader to my own manuscript remarks on the weights, coins, and measures of the ancients, which were abruptly terminated by the militia drum.

As I am now entering on a more ample field of society and study, I can only hope to avoid a vain and prolix garrulity, by overlooking the vulgar crowd of my acquaintance, and confining myself to such intimate friends among books and men, as are best entitled to my notice by their own merit and reputation, or by the deep impression which they have left on my mind. Yet I will embrace this occasion of recommending to the young student a practice, which about this time I myself adopted. After glancing my eye over the design and order of a new book, I suspended the perusal till I had finished the task of self examination, till I had revolved, in a solitary walk, all that I knew or believed, or had thought on the subject of the whole work, or of some particular chapter: I was then qualified to discern how much the author added to my original stock; and I was sometimes satisfied by the agreement, I was sometimes armed by the opposition of our ideas. The favourite companions of my leisure were our English writers since the Revolution: they breathe the spirit of reason and liberty; and they most seasonably contributed to restore the purity of my own language, which had been corrupted by the long use of a foreign idiom. By the judicious advice of Mr. Mallet, I was directed to the writings of Swift and Addison; wit and simplicity are their common attributes: but the style of Swift is supported by manly original vigour; that of Addison is adorned by the female graces of elegance and mildness. The old reproach, that no British altars had been raised to the muse of history, was recently disproved by the first performances of Robertson and Hume, the histories of Scotland and of the Stuarts. I will assume the presumption of saying, that I was not unworthy to read them: nor will I disguise my different feelings in the repeated perusals. The perfect composition, the nervous language, the well-turned periods of Dr. Robertson, inflamed me to the ambitious hope that I might one day tread in his footsteps: the calm philosophy, the careless, inimitable beauties of his friend and rival, often forced me to close the volume with a mixed sensation of delight and despair.

The design of my first work, the Essay on the Study of Literature, was suggested by a refinement of vanity, the desire of justifying and praising the object of a favourite pursuit. In France, to which my ideas were confined, the learning and language of Greece and Rome were neglected by a philosophic age. The guardian of those studies, the Academy of Inscriptions, was degraded to the lowest rank among the three royal societies of Paris: the new appellation of Erudits was contemptuously applied to the successors of Lipsius and Casaubon; and I was provoked to hear (see M. d'Alembert Discours preliminaire a l'Encyclopedie) that the exercise of the memory, their sole merit, had been superseded by the nobler faculties of the imagination and the judgment. I was ambitious of proving by my own example, as well as by my precepts, that all the faculties of the mind may be exercised and displayed by the study of ancient literature: I began to select and adorn the various proofs and illustrations which had offered themselves in reading the classics; and the first pages or chapters of my essay were composed before my departure from Lausanne. The hurry of the journey, and of the first weeks of my English life, suspended all thoughts of serious application: but my object was ever before my eyes; and no more than ten days, from the first to the eleventh of July, were suffered to elapse after my summer establishment at Buriton. My essay was finished in about six weeks; and as soon as a fair copy had been transcribed by one of the French prisoners at Petersfield, I looked round for a critic and judge of my first performance. A writer can seldom be content with the doubtful recompense of solitary approbation; but a youth ignorant of the world, and of himself, must desire to weigh his talents in some scales less partial than his own: my conduct was natural, my motive laudable, my choice of Dr. Maty judicious and fortunate. By descent and education Dr. Maty, though born in Holland, might be considered as a Frenchman; but he was fixed in London by the practice of physic, and an office in the British Museum. His reputation was justly founded on the eighteen volumes of the Journal Britannique, which he had supported, almost alone, with perseverance and success. This humble though useful labour, which had once been dignified by the genius of Bayle and the learning of Le Clerc, was not disgraced by the taste, the knowledge, and the judgment of Maty: he exhibits a candid and pleasing view of the state of literature in England during a period of six years (January 1750—December 1755); and, far different from his angry son, he handles the rod of criticism with the tenderness and reluctance of a parent. The author of the Journal Britannique sometimes aspires to the character of a poet and philosopher: his style is pure and elegant; and in his virtues, or even in his defects, he may be ranked as one of the last disciples of the school of Fontenelle. His answer to my first letter was prompt and polite: after a careful examination he returned my manuscript, with some animadversion and much applause; and when I visited London in the ensuing winter, we discussed the design and execution in several free and familiar conversations. In a short excursion to Buriton I reviewed my essay, according to his friendly advice; and after suppressing a third, adding a third, and altering a third, I consummated my first labour by a short preface, which is dated Feb. 3, 1759. Yet I still shrunk from the press with the terrors of virgin modesty: the manuscript was safely deposited in my desk; and as my attention was engaged by new objects, the delay might have been prolonged till I had fulfilled the precept of Horace, "nonumque prematur in annum." Father Sirmond, a learned jesuit, was still more rigid, since he advised a young friend to expect the mature age of fifty, before he gave himself or his writings to the public (Olivet Hist. de l'Acad. Francoise, tom. ii. p. 143). The counsel was singular; but it is still more singular that it should have been approved by the example of the author. Sirmond was himself fifty-five years of age when he published (in 1614) his first work, an edition of Sidonius Apollinaris, with many valuable annotations: (see his life, before the great edition of his works in five volumes folio, Paris, 1696, e Typographia Regia).

Two years elapsed in silence: but in the spring of 1761 I yielded to the authority of a parent, and complied, like a pious son, with the wish of my own heart. My private resolves were influenced by the state of Europe. About this time the belligerent powers had made and accepted overtures of peace; our English plenipotentiaries were named to assist at the Congress of Augsburg, which never met: I wished to attend them as a gentleman or a secretary; and my father fondly believed that the proof of some literary talents might introduce me to public notice, and second the recommendations of my friends. After a last revisal I consulted with Mr. Mallet and Dr. Maty, who approved the design and promoted the execution. Mr. Mallet, after hearing me read my manuscript, received it from my hands, and delivered it into those of Becket, with whom he made an agreement in my name; an easy agreement: I required only a certain number of copies; and, without transferring my property, I devolved on the bookseller the charges and profits of the edition. Dr. Maty undertook, in my absence, to correct the sheets: he inserted, without my knowledge, an elegant and flattering epistle to the author; which is composed, however, with so much art, that, in case of a defeat, his favourable report might have been ascribed to the indulgence of a friend for the rash attempt of a young English gentleman. The work was printed and published, under the title of Essai sur l'Etude de la Litterature, a Londres, chez T. Becket et P. A. de Hondt, 1761, in a small volume in duodecimo: my dedication to my father, a proper and pious address, was composed the twenty-eighth of May: Dr. Maty's letter is dated June 16; and I received the first copy (June 23) at Alresford, two days before I marched with the Hampshire militia. Some weeks afterwards, on the same ground, I presented my book to the late Duke of York, who breakfasted in Colonel Pitt's tent. By my father's direction, and Mallet's advice, many literary gifts were distributed to several eminent characters in England and France; two books were sent to the Count de Caylus, and the Duchesse d'Aiguillon, at Paris: I had reserved twenty copies for my friends at Lausanne, as the first fruits of my education, and a grateful token of my remembrance: and on all these persons I levied an unavoidable tax of civility and compliment. It is not surprising that a work, of which the style and sentiments were so totally foreign, should have been more successful abroad than at home. I was delighted by the copious extracts, the warm commendations, and the flattering predictions of the journals of France and Holland: and the next year (1762) a new edition (I believe at Geneva) extended the fame, or at least the circulation, of the work. In England it was received with cold indifference, little read, and speedily forgotten: a small impression was slowly dispersed; the bookseller murmured, and the author (had his feelings been more exquisite) might have wept over the blunders and baldness of the English translation. The publication of my History fifteen years afterwards revived the memory of my first performance, and the Essay was eagerly sought in the shops. But I refused the permission which Becket solicited of reprinting it: the public curiosity was imperfectly satisfied by a pirated copy of the booksellers of Dublin; and when a copy of the original edition has been discovered in a sale, the primitive value of half-a-crown has risen to the fanciful price of a guinea or thirty shillings.

I have expatiated on the petty circumstances and period of my first publication, a memorable aera in the life of a student, when he ventures to reveal the measure of his mind: his hopes and fears are multiplied by the idea of self-importance, and he believes for a while that the eyes of mankind are fixed on his person and performance. Whatever may be my present reputation, it no longer rests on the merit of this first essay; and at the end of twenty-eight years I may appreciate my juvenile work with the impartiality, and almost with the indifference, of a stranger. In his answer to Lady Hervey, the Count de Caylus admires, or affects to admire, "les livres sans nombre que Mr. Gibbon a lus et tres bien lus." But, alas! my stock of erudition at that time was scanty and superficial; and if I allow myself the liberty of naming the Greek masters, my genuine and personal acquaintance was confined to the Latin classics. The most serious defect of my Essay is a kind of obscurity and abruptness which always fatigues, and may often elude, the attention of the reader. Instead of a precise and proper definition of the title itself, the sense of the word Litterature is loosely and variously applied: a number of remarks and examples, historical, critical, philosophical, are heaped on each other without method or connection; and if we except some introductory pages, all the remaining chapters might indifferently be reversed or transposed. The obscure passages is often affected, brevis esse laboro, obscurus fio; the desire of expressing perhaps a common idea with sententious and oracular brevity: alas! how fatal has been the imitation of Montesquieu! But this obscurity sometimes proceeds from a mixture of light and darkness in the author's mind; from a partial ray which strikes upon an angle, instead of spreading itself over the surface of an object. After this fair confession I shall presume to say, that the Essay does credit to a young writer of two and twenty years of age, who had read with taste, who thinks with freedom, and who writes in a foreign language with spirit and elegance. The defence of the early History of Rome and the new Chronology of Sir Isaac Newton form a specious argument. The patriotic and political design of the Georgics is happily conceived; and any probable conjecture, which tends to raise the dignity of the poet and the poem, deserves to be adopted, without a rigid scrutiny. Some dawnings of a philosophic spirit enlighten the general remarks on the study of history and of man. I am not displeased with the inquiry into the origin and nature of the gods of polytheism, which might deserve the illustration of a riper judgment. Upon the whole, I may apply to the first labour of my pen the speech of a far superior artist, when be surveyed the first productions of his pencil. After viewing some portraits which he had painted in his youth, my friend Sir Joshua Reynolds acknowledged to me, that he was rather humbled than flattered by the comparison with his present works; and that after so much time and study, he had conceived his improvement to be much greater than he found it to have been.

At Lausanne I composed the first chapters of my Essay in French, the familiar language of my conversation and studies, in which it was easier for me to write than in my mother tongue. After my return to England I continued the same practice, without any affectation, or design of repudiating (as Dr. Bentley would say) my vernacular idiom. But I should have escaped some Anti-gallican clamour, had I been content with the more natural character of an English author. I should have been more consistent had I rejected Mallet's advice, of prefixing an English dedication to a French book; a confusion of tongues that seemed to accuse the ignorance of my patron. The use of a foreign dialect might be excused by the hope of being employed as a negociator, by the desire of being generally understood on the continent; but my true motive was doubtless the ambition of new and singular fame, an Englishman claiming a place among the writers of France. The latin tongue had been consecrated by the service of the church, it was refined by the imitation of the ancients; and in the fifteenth and sixteenth centuries the scholars of Europe enjoyed the advantage, which they have gradually resigned, of conversing and writing in a common and learned idiom. As that idiom was no longer in any country the vulgar speech, they all stood on a level with each other; yet a citizen of old Rome might have smiled at the best Latinity of the Germans and Britons; and we may learn from the Ciceronianus of Erasmus, how difficult it was found to steer a middle course between pedantry and barbarism. The Romans themselves had sometimes attempted a more perilous task, of writing in a living language, and appealing to the taste and judgment of the natives. The vanity of Tully was doubly interested in the Greek memoirs of his own consulship; and if he modestly supposes that some Latinisms might be detected in his style, he is confident of his own skill in the art of Isocrates and Aristotle; and he requests his friend Atticus to disperse the copies of his work at Athens, and in the other cities of Greece, (Ad Atticum, i. 19. ii. i.) But it must not be forgotten, that from infancy to manhood Cicero and his contemporaries had read and declaimed, and composed with equal diligence in both languages; and that he was not allowed to frequent a Latin school till he had imbibed the lessons of the Greek grammarians and rhetoricians. In modern times, the language of France has been diffused by the merit of her writers, the social manners of the natives, the influence of the monarchy, and the exile of the protestants. Several foreigners have seized the opportunity of speaking to Europe in this common dialect, and Germany may plead the authority of Leibnitz and Frederick, of the first of her philosophers, and the greatest of her kings. The just pride and laudable prejudice of England has restrained this communication of idioms; and of all the nations on this side of the Alps, my Countrymen are the least practised, and least perfect in the exercise of the French tongue. By Sir William Temple and Lord Chesterfield it was only used on occasions of civility and business, and their printed letters will not be quoted as models of composition. Lord Bolingbroke may have published in French a sketch of his Reflections on Exile: but his reputation now reposes on the address of Voltaire, "Docte sermones utriusque linguae;" and by his English dedication to Queen Caroline, and his Essay on Epic Poetry, it should seem that Voltaire himself wished to deserve a return of the same compliment. The exception of Count Hamilton cannot fairly be urged; though an Irishman by birth, he was educated in France from his childhood. Yet I am surprised that a long residence in England, and the habits of domestic conversation, did not affect the ease and purity of his inimitable style; and I regret the omission of his English verses, which might have afforded an amusing object of comparison. I might therefore assume the primus ego in patriam, &c.; but with what success I have explored this untrodden path must be left to the decision of my French readers. Dr. Maty, who might himself be questioned as a foreigner, has secured his retreat at my expense. "Je ne crois pas que vous vous piquiez d'etre moins facile a reconnoitre pour un Anglois que Lucullus pour un Romain." My friends at Paris have been more indulgent, they received me as a countryman, or at least as a provincial; but they were friends and Parisians. The defects which Maty insinuates, "Ces traits saillans, ces figures hardies, ce sacrifice de la regle au sentiment, et de la cadence a la force," are the faults of the youth, rather than of the stranger: and after the long and laborious exercise of my own language, I am conscious that my French style has been ripened and improved.

I have already hinted, that the publication of my essay was delayed till I had embraced the military profession. I shall now amuse myself with the recollection of an active scene, which bears no affinity to any other period of my studious and social life.

In the outset of a glorious war, the English people had been defended by the aid of German mercenaries. A national militia has been the cry of every patriot since the Revolution; and this measure, both in parliament and in the field, was supported by the country gentlemen or Tories, who insensibly transferred their loyalty to the house of Hanover: in the language of Mr. Burke, they have changed the idol, but they have preserved the idolatry. In the act of offering our names and receiving our commissions, as major and captain in the Hampshire regiment, (June 12, 1759,) we had not supposed that we should be dragged away, my father from his farm, myself from my books, and condemned, during two years and a half, (May 10, 1760—December 23, 1762,) to a wandering life of military servitude. But a weekly or monthly exercise of thirty thousand provincials would have left them useless and ridiculous; and after the pretence of an invasion had vanished, the popularity of Mr. Pitt gave a sanction to the illegal step of keeping them till the end of the war under arms, in constant pay and duty, and at a distance from their respective homes. When the King's order for our embodying came down, it was too late to retreat, and too soon to repent. The South battalion of the Hampshire militia was a small independent corps of four hundred and seventy-six, officers and men, commanded by lieutenant-colonel Sir Thomas Worsley, who, after a prolix and passionate contest, delivered us from the tyranny of the lord lieutenant, the Duke of Bolton. My proper station, as first captain, was at the head of my own, and afterwards of the grenadier, company; but in the absence, or even in the presence, of the two field officers, I was entrusted by my friend and my father with the effective labour of dictating the orders, and exercising the battalion. With the help of an original journal, I could write the history of my bloodless and inglorious campaigns; but as these events have lost much of their importance in my own eyes, they shall be dispatched in a few words. From Winchester, the first place of assembly, (June 4, 1760,) we were removed, at our own request, for the benefit of a foreign education. By the arbitrary, and often capricious, orders of the War-office, the battalion successively marched to the pleasant and hospitable Blandford (June 17); to Hilsea barracks, a seat of disease and discord (Sept. 1); to Cranbrook in the weald of Kent (Dec. 11); to the sea-coast of Dover (Dec. 27); to Winchester camp (June 25, 1761); to the populous and disorderly town of Devizes (Oct. 23); to Salisbury (Feb. 28, 1762); to our beloved Blandford a second time (March 9); and finally, to the fashionable resort of Southampton (June 2); where the colours were fixed till our final dissolution. (Dec. 23). On the beach at Dover we had exercised in sight of the Gallic shores. But the most splendid and useful scene of our life was a four months' encampment on Winchester Down, under the command of the Earl of Effingham. Our army consisted of the thirty-fourth regiment of foot and six militia corps. The consciousness of our defects was stimulated by friendly emulation. We improved our time and opportunities in morning and evening field-days; and in the general reviews the South Hampshire were rather a credit than a disgrace to the line. In our subsequent quarters of the Devizes and

Blandford, we advanced with a quick step in our military studies; the ballot of the ensuing summer renewed our vigour and youth; and had the militia subsisted another year, we might have contested the prize with the most perfect of our brethren.

The loss of so many busy and idle hours was not compensated by any elegant pleasure; and my temper was insensibly soured by the society of out rustic officers. In every state there exists, however, a balance of good and evil. The habits of a sedentary life were usefully broken by the duties of an active profession: in the healthful exercise of the field I hunted with a battalion, instead of a pack; and at that time I was ready, at any hour of the day or night, to fly from quarters to London, from London to quarters, on the slightest call of private or regimental business. But my principal obligation to the militia, was the making me an Englishman, and a soldier. After my foreign education, with my reserved temper, I should long have continued a stranger in my native country, had I not been shaken in this various scene of new faces and new friends: had not experience forced me to feel the characters of our leading men, the state of parties, the forms of office, and the operation of our civil and military system. In this peaceful service I imbibed the rudiments of the language, and science of tactics, which opened a new field of study and observation. I diligently read, and meditated, the Memoires Militaires of Quintus Icilius, (Mr. Guichardt,) the only writer who has united the merits of a professor and a veteran. The discipline and evolutions of a modern battalion gave me a clearer notion of the phalanx and the legion; and the captain of the Hampshire grenadiers (the reader may smile) has not been useless to the historian of the Roman empire.

A youth of any spirit is fired even by the play of arms, and in the first sallies of my enthusiasm I had seriously attempted to embrace the regular profession of a soldier. But this military fever was cooled by the enjoyment of our mimic Bellona, who soon unveiled to my eyes her naked deformity. How often did I sigh for my proper station in society and letters. How often (a proud comparison) did I repeat the complaint of Cicero in the command of a provincial army: "Clitellae bovi sunt impositae. Est incredibile quam me negotii taedeat. Non habet satis magnum campum ille tibi non ignotus cursus animi; et industriae meae praeclara opera cessat. Lucem, libros, urbem, domum, vos desidero. Sed feram, ut potero;

sit modo annuum. Si prorogatur, actum est."—Epist. ad Atticum, lib. v. 15. From a service without danger I might indeed have retired without disgrace; but as often as I hinted a wish of resigning, my fetters were riveted by the friendly intreaties of the colonel, the parental authority of the major, and my own regard for the honour and welfare of the battalion. When I felt that my personal escape was impracticable, I bowed my neck to the yoke: my servitude was protracted far beyond the annual patience of Cicero; and it was not till after the preliminaries of peace that I received my discharge, from the act of government which disembodied the militia.

When I complain of the loss of time, justice to myself and to the militia must throw the greatest part of that reproach on the first seven or eight months, while I was obliged to learn as well as to teach. The dissipation of Blandford, and the disputes of Portsmouth, consumed the hours which were not employed in the field; and amid the perpetual hurry of an inn, a barrack, or a guard-room, all literary ideas were banished from my mind. After this long fast, the longest which I have ever known, I once more tasted at Dover the pleasures of reading and thinking; and the hungry appetite with which I opened a volume of Tully's philosophical works is still present to my memory. The last review of my Essay before its publication, had prompted me to investigate the nature of the gods; my inquiries led me to the Historie Critique du Manicheisme of Beausobre, who discusses many deep questions of Pagan and Christian theology: and from this rich treasury of facts and opinions, I deduced my own consequences, beyond the holy circle of the author. After this recovery I never relapsed into indolence; and my example might prove, that in the life most averse to study, some hours may be stolen, some minutes may be snatched. Amidst the tumult of Winchester camp I sometimes thought and read in my tent; in the more settled quarters of the Devizes, Blandford, and Southampton, I always secured a separate lodging, and the necessary books; and in the summer of 1762, while the new militia was raising, I enjoyed at Buriton two or three months of literary repose. In forming a new plan of study, I hesitated between the mathematics and the Greek language; both of which I had neglected since my return from Lausanne. I consulted a learned and friendly mathematician, Mr. George Scott, a pupil of de Moivre; and his map of a country which I have never explored, may perhaps be more serviceable to others. As soon as I had given the preference to Greek, the example of Scaliger and my own reason determined me on the choice of Homer, the father of poetry, and the Bible of the ancients: but Scaliger ran through the Iliad in one and twenty days; and I was not dissatisfied with my own diligence for performing the same labour in an equal number of weeks. After the first difficulties were surmounted, the language of nature and harmony soon became easy and familiar, and each day I sailed upon the ocean with a brisker gale and a more steady course.

{Passage in Greek}

Ilias, A 481.
> —Fair wind, and blowing fresh,
> Apollo sent them; quick they rear'd the mast,
> Then spread th'unsullied canvas to the gale,
> And the wind fill'd it. Roar'd the sable flood
> Around the bark, that ever as she went
> Dash'd wide the brine, and scudded swift away.
> COWPER'S Homer.

In the study of a poet who has since become the most intimate of my friends, I successively applied many passages and fragments of Greek writers; and among these I shall notice a life of Homer, in the Oposcula Mythologica of Gale, several books of the geography of Strabo, and the entire treatise of Longinus, which, from the title and the style, is equally worthy of the epithet of sublime. My grammatical skill was improved, my vocabulary was enlarged; and in the militia I acquired a just and indelible knowledge of the first of languages. On every march, in every journey, Horace was always in my pocket, and often in my hand: but I should not mention his two critical epistles, the amusement of a morning, had they not been accompanied by the elaborate commentary of Dr. Hurd, now Bishop of Worcester. On the interesting subjects of composition and imitation of epic and dramatic poetry, I presumed to think for myself; and thirty close-written pages in folio could scarcely comprise my full and free discussion of the sense of the master and the pedantry of the servant.

After his oracle Dr. Johnson, my friend Sir Joshua Reynolds denies all original genius, any natural propensity of the mind to one art or science rather than another. Without engaging in a metaphysical or rather verbal dispute, I know, by experience, that from my early youth I aspired to the character of an historian. While I served in the militia, before and after the publication of my essay, this idea ripened in my mind; nor can I paint in more lively colours the feelings of the moment, than by transcribing some passages, under their respective dates, from a journal which I kept at that time. Beriton, April 14, 1761. (In a short excursion from Dover.)— "Having thought of several subjects for an historical composition, I chose the expedition of Charles VIII. of France into Italy. I read two memoirs of Mr. de Foncemagne in the Academy of Inscriptions (tom. xvii. p. 539-607.), and abstracted them. I likewise finished this day a dissertation, in which I examine the right of Charles VIII. to the crown of Naples, and the rival claims of the House of Anjou and Arragon: it consists of ten folio pages, besides large notes."

Beriton, August 4, 1761. (In a week's excursion from Winchester camp.)—"After having long revolved subjects for my intended historical essay, I renounced my first thought of the expedition of Charles VIII. as too remote from us, and rather an introduction to great events, than great and important in itself. I successively chose and rejected the crusade of Richard the First, the barons' wars against John and Henry the Third, the History of Edward the Black Prince, the lives and comparisons of Henry V. and the Emperor Titus, the life of Sir Philip Sidney, and that of the Marquis of Montrose. At length I have fixed on Sir Walter Raleigh for my hero. His eventful story is varied by the characters of the soldier and sailor, the courtier and historian; and it may afford such a fund of materials as I desire, which have not yet been properly manufactured. At present I cannot attempt the execution of this work. Free leisure, and the opportunity of consulting many books, both printed and manuscript, are as necessary as they are impossible to be attained in my present way of life. However, to acquire a general insight into my subject and resources, I read the life of Sir Walter Raleigh by Dr. Birch, his copious article in the General Dictionary by the same hand, and the reigns of Queen Elizabeth and James the First in Hume's History of England." Beriton, January 1762. (In a month's absence from the Devizes.)—

"During this interval of repose, I again turned my thoughts to Sir Walter Raleigh, and looked more closely into my materials. I read the two volumes in quarto of the Bacon Papers, published by Dr. Birch; the Fragmenta Regalia of Sir Robert Naunton, Mallet's Life of Lord Bacon, and the political treatises of that great man in the first volume of his works, with many of his letters in the second; Sir William Monson's Naval Tracts, and the elaborate life of Sir Walter Raleigh, which Mr. Oldys has prefixed to the best edition of his History of the World. My subject opens upon me, and in general improves upon a nearer prospect."

Beriton, July 26, 1762. (During my summer residence.)—"I am afraid of being reduced to drop my hero; but my time has not, however, been lost in the research of his story, and of a memorable aera of our English annals. The life of Sir Walter Raleigh, by Oldys, is a very poor performance; a servile panegyric, or flat apology, tediously minute, and composed in a dull and affected style. Yet the author was a man of diligence and learning, who had read everything relative to his subject, and whose ample collections are arranged with perspicuity and method. Excepting some anecdotes lately revealed in the Sidney and Bacon Papers, I know not what I should be able to add. My ambition (exclusive of the uncertain merit of style and sentiment) must be confined to the hope of giving a good abridgment of Oldys. I have even the disappointment of finding some parts of this copious work very dry and barren; and these parts are unluckily some of the most characteristic: Raleigh's colony of Virginia, his quarrels with Essex, the true secret of his conspiracy, and, above all, the detail of his private life, the most essential and important to a biographer. My best resource would be in the circumjacent history of the times, and perhaps in some digressions artfully introduced, like the fortunes of the Peripatetic philosophy in the portrait of Lord Bacon. But the reigns of Elizabeth and James the First are the periods of English history, which have been the most variously illustrated: and what new lights could I reflect on a subject, which has exercised the accurate industry of Birch, the lively and curious acuteness of Walpole, the critical spirit of Hurd, the vigorous sense of Mallet and Robertson, and the impartial philosophy of Hume? Could I even surmount these obstacles, I should shrink with terror from the modern history of England, where every character is a problem, and every reader a friend or an enemy; where a writer is supposed to hoist a flag of party, and is devoted to damnation by the adverse faction. Such would be my reception at home: and abroad, the historian of Raleigh must encounter an indifference far more bitter than censure or reproach. The events of his life are interesting: but his character is ambiguous, his actions are obscure, his writings are English, and his fame is confined to the narrow limits of our language and our island. I must embrace a safer and more extensive theme.

"There is one which I should prefer to all others, The History of the Liberty of the Swiss, of that independence which a brave people rescued from the House of Austria, defended against a Dauphin of France, and finally sealed with the blood of Charles of Burgundy. From such a theme, so full of public spirit, of military glory, of examples of virtue, of lessons of government, the dullest stranger would catch fire; what might not I hope, whose talents, whatsoever they may be, would be inflamed with the zeal of patriotism. But the materials of this history are inaccessible to me, fast locked in the obscurity of an old barbarous German dialect, of which I am totally ignorant, and which I cannot resolve to learn for this sole and peculiar purpose.

"I have another subject in view, which is the contrast of the former history: the one a poor, warlike, virtuous republic, which emerges into glory and freedom; the other a commonwealth, soft, opulent, and corrupt; which, by just degrees, is precipitated from the abuse to the loss of her liberty: both lessons are, perhaps, equally instructive. This second subject is, The History of the Republic of Florence under the House of Medicis: a period of one hundred and fifty years, which rises or descends from the dregs of the Florentine democracy, to the title and dominion of Cosmo de Medicis in the Grand Duchy of Tuscany. I might deduce a chain of revolutions not unworthy of the pen of Vertot; singular men, and singular events; the Medicis four times expelled, and as often recalled; and the Genius of Freedom reluctantly yielding to the arms of Charles V. and the policy of Cosmo. The character and fate of Savanerola, and the revival of arts and letters in Italy, will be essentially connected with the elevation of the family and the fall of the republic. The Medicis (stirps quasi fataliter nata ad instauranda vel fovenda studia (Lipsius ad Germanos et Galles, Epist. viii.)) were illustrated by the patronage of learning; and enthusiasm was the most formidable weapon of their adversaries. On this splendid subject I shall most probably fix; but when, or where, or how will it be executed? I behold in a dark and doubtful perspective."

Res alta terra, et caligine mersas.

The youthful habits of the language and manners of France had left in my mind an ardent desire of revisiting the Continent on a larger and more liberal plan. According to the law of custom, and perhaps of reason, foreign travel completes the education of an English gentleman: my father had consented to my wish, but I was detained above four years by my rash engagement in the militia. I eagerly grasped the first moments of freedom: three or four weeks in Hampshire and London were employed in the preparations of my journey, and the farewell visits of friendship and civility: my last act in town was to applaud Mallet's new tragedy of Elvira; a post-chaise conveyed me to Dover, the packet to Boulogne, and such was my diligence, that I reached Paris on Jan. 28, 1763, only thirty-six days after the disbanding of the militia. Two or three years were loosely defined for the term of my absence; and I was left at liberty to spend that time in such places and in such a manner as was most agreeable to my taste and judgment.

In this first visit I passed three months and a half, (Jan. 28-May 9,) and a much longer space might have been agreeably filled, without any intercourse with the natives. At home we are content to move in the daily round of pleasure and business; and a scene which is always present is supposed to be within our knowledge, or at least within our power. But in a foreign country, curiosity is our business and our pleasure; and the traveller, conscious of his ignorance, and covetous of his time, is diligent in the search and the view of every object that can deserve his attention. I devoted many hours of the morning to the circuit of Paris and the neighbourhood, to the visit of churches and palaces conspicuous by their architecture, to the royal manufactures, collections of books and pictures, and all the various treasures of art, of learning, and of luxury. An Englishman may hear without reluctance, that in these curious and costly articles Paris is superior to London; since the opulence of the French capital arises from the defects of its government and religion. In the absence of Louis XIV. and his successors, the Louvre has been left unfinished: but the millions which have been lavished on the sands of Versailles, and the morass of Marli, could not be supplied by the legal allowance of a British king. The splendour of the French nobles is confined to their town residence; that of the English is more usefully distributed in their country seats; and we should be astonished at our own riches, if the labours of architecture, the spoils of Italy and Greece, which are now scattered from Inverary to Wilton, were accumulated in a few streets between Marylebone and Westminster. All superfluous ornament is rejected by the cold frugality of the protestants; but the catholic superstition, which is always the enemy of reason, is often the parent of the arts. The wealthy communities of priests and monks expend their revenues in stately edifices; and the parish church of St. Sulpice, one of the noblest structures in Paris, was built and adorned by the private industry of a late cure. In this outset, and still more in the sequel of my tour, my eye was amused; but the pleasing vision cannot be fixed by the pen; the particular images are darkly seen through the medium of five-and-twenty years, and the narrative of my life must not degenerate into a book of travels.

But the principal end of my journey was to enjoy the society of a polished and amiable people, in whose favour I was strongly prejudiced, and to converse with some authors, whose conversation, as I fondly imagined, must be far more pleasing and instructive than their writings. The moment was happily chosen. At the close of a successful war the British name was respected on the continent.

Clarum et venerabile nomen
Gentibus.

Our opinions, our fashions, even our games, were adopted in France, a ray of national glory illuminated each individual, and every Englishman was supposed to be born a patriot and a philosopher. For myself, I carried a personal recommendation; my name and my Essay were already known; the compliment of having written in the French language entitled me to some returns of civility and gratitude. I was considered as a man of letters, who wrote for amusement. Before my departure I had obtained from the Duke de Nivernois, Lady Hervey, the Mallets, Mr. Walpole, &c. many letters of recommendation to their private or literary friends.

Of these epistles the reception and success were determined by the character and situation of the persons by whom and to whom they were addressed: the seed was sometimes cast on a barren rock, and it sometimes multiplied an hundred fold in the production of new shoots, spreading branches, and exquisite fruit. But upon the whole, I had reason to praise the national urbanity, which from the court has diffused its gentle influence to the shop, the cottage, and the schools. Of the men of genius of the age, Montesquieu and Fontenelle were no more; Voltaire resided on his own estate near Geneva; Rousseau in the preceding year had been driven from his hermitage of Montmorency; and I blush at my having neglected to seek, in this journey, the acquaintance of Buffon. Among the men of letters whom I saw, D'Alembert and Diderot held the foremost rank in merit, or at least in fame. I shall content myself with enumerating the well-known names of the Count de Caylus, of the Abbe de la Bleterie, Barthelemy, Reynal, Arnaud, of Messieurs de la Condamine, du Clos, de Ste Palaye, de Bougainville, Caperonnier, de Guignes, Suard, &c. without attempting to discriminate the shades of their characters, or the degrees of our connection. Alone, in a morning visit, I commonly found the artists and authors of Paris less vain, and more reasonable, than in the circles of their equals, with whom they mingle in the houses of the rich. Four days in a week, I had place, without invitation, at the hospitable tables of Mesdames Geoffrin and du Bocage, of the celebrated Helvetius, and of the Baron d'Olbach. In these symposia the pleasures of the table were improved by lively and liberal conversation; the company was select, though various and voluntary.

The society of Madame du Bocage was more soft and moderate than that of her rivals, and the evening conversations of M. de Foncemagne were supported by the good sense and learning of the principal members of the Academy of Inscriptions. The opera and the Italians I occasionally visited; but the French theatre, both in tragedy and comedy, was my daily and favourite amusement. Two famous actresses then divided the public applause. For my own part, I preferred the consummate art of the Claron, to the intemperate sallies of the Dumesnil, which were extolled by her admirers, as the genuine voice of nature and passion. Fourteen weeks insensibly stole away; but had I been rich and independent,

I should have prolonged, and perhaps have fixed, my residence at Paris.

Between the expensive style of Paris and of Italy it was prudent to interpose some months of tranquil simplicity; and at the thoughts of Lausanne I again lived in the pleasures and studies of my early youth. Shaping my course through Dijon and Besancon, in the last of which places I was kindly entertained by my cousin Acton, I arrived in the month of May 1763 on the banks of the Leman Lake. It had been my intention to pass the Alps in the autumn, but such are the simple attractions of the place, that the year had almost expired before my departure from Lausanne in the ensuing spring. An absence of five years had not made much alteration in manners, or even in persons. My old friends, of both sexes, hailed my voluntary return; the most genuine proof of my attachment. They had been flattered by the present of my book, the produce of their soil; and the good Pavilliard shed tears of joy as he embraced a pupil, whose literary merit he might fairly impute to his own labours. To my old list I added some new acquaintance, and among the strangers I shall distinguish Prince Lewis of Wirtemberg, the brother of the reigning Duke, at whose country-house, near Lausanne, I frequently dined: a wandering meteor, and at length a falling star, his light and ambitious spirit had successively dropped from the firmament of Prussia, of France, and of Austria; and his faults, which he styled his misfortunes, had driven him into philosophic exile in the Pays de Vaud. He could now moralize on the vanity of the world, the equality of mankind, and the happiness of a private station. His address was affable and polite, and as he had shone in courts and armies, his memory could supply, and his eloquence could adorn, a copious fund of interesting anecdotes. His first enthusiasm was that of charity and agriculture; but the sage gradually lapsed in the saint, and Prince Lewis of Wirtemberg is now buried in a hermitage near Mayence, in the last stage of mystic devotion. By some ecclesiastical quarrel, Voltaire had been provoked to withdraw himself from Lausanne, and retire to his castle at Ferney, where I again visited the poet and the actor, without seeking his more intimate acquaintance, to which I might now have pleaded a better title. But the theatre which he had founded, the actors whom he had formed, survived the loss of their master; and, recent from Paris, I attended with pleasure at the representation of several tragedies and comedies. I shall not descend to specify particular names and characters; but I cannot forget a private institution, which will display the innocent freedom of Swiss manners. My favourite society had assumed, from the age of its members, the proud denomination of the spring (la society du printems). It consisted of fifteen or twenty young unmarried ladies, of genteel, though not of the very first families; the eldest perhaps about twenty, all agreeable, several handsome, and two or three of exquisite beauty. At each other's houses they assembled almost every day, without the controul, or even the presence, of a mother or an aunt; they were trusted to their own prudence, among a crowd of young men of every nation in Europe. They laughed, they sung, they danced, they played at cards, they acted comedies; but in the midst of this careless gaiety, they respected themselves, and were respected by the men; the invisible line between liberty and licentiousness was never transgressed by a gesture, a word, or a look, and their virgin chastity was never sullied by the breath of scandal or suspicion. A singular institution, expressive of the innocent simplicity of Swiss manners. After having tasted the luxury of England and Paris, I could not have returned with satisfaction to the coarse and homely table of Madame Pavilliard; nor was her husband offended that I now entered myself as a pensionaire, or boarder, in the elegant house of Mr. De Mesery, which may be entitled to a short remembrance, as it has stood above twenty years, perhaps, without a parallel in Europe. The house in which we lodged was spacious and convenient, in the best street, and commanding, from behind, a noble prospect over the country and the Lake. Our table was served with neatness and plenty; the boarders were select; we had the liberty of inviting any guests at a stated price; and in the summer the scene was occasionally transferred to a pleasant villa, about a league from Lausanne. The characters of Master and Mistress were happily suited to each other, and to their situation. At the age of seventy-five, Madame de Mesery, who has survived her husband, is still a graceful, I had almost said, a handsome woman. She was alike qualified to preside in her kitchen and her drawing-room; and such was the equal propriety of her conduct, that of two or three hundred foreigners, none ever failed in respect, none could complain of her neglect, and none could ever boast of her favour. Mesery himself, of the noble family of De Crousaz, was a man of the world, a jovial companion, whose easy manners and natural sallies maintained the cheerfulness of his house. His wit could laugh at his own ignorance: he disguised, by an air of profusion, a strict attention to his interest; and in this situation he appeared like a nobleman who spent his fortune and entertained his friends. In this agreeable society I resided nearly eleven months (May 1763—April 1764); and in this second visit to Lausanne, among a crowd of my English companions, I knew and esteemed Mr. Holroyd (now Lord Sheffield); and our mutual attachment was renewed and fortified in the subsequent stages of our Italian journey. Our lives are in the power of chance, and a slight variation on either side, in time or place, might have deprived me of a friend, whose activity in the ardour of youth was always prompted by a benevolent heart, and directed by a strong understanding.

If my studies at Paris had been confined to the study of the world, three or four months would not have been unprofitably spent. My visits, however superficial, to the Academy of Medals and the public libraries, opened a new field of inquiry; and the view of so many manuscripts of different ages and characters induced me to consult the two great Benedictine works, the Diplomatica of Mabillon, and the Palaeographia of Montfaucon. I studied the theory without attaining the practice of the art: nor should I complain of the intricacy of Greek abbreviations and Gothic alphabets, since every day, in a familiar language, I am at a loss to decipher the hieroglyphics of a female note. In a tranquil scene, which revived the memory of my first studies, idleness would have been less pardonable: the public libraries of Lausanne and Geneva liberally supplied me with books; and if many hours were lost in dissipation, many more were employed in literary labour. In the country, Horace and Virgil, Juvenal and Ovid, were my assiduous companions but, in town, I formed and executed a plan of study for the use of my Transalpine expedition: the topography of old Rome, the ancient geography of Italy, and the science of medals. 1. I diligently read, almost always with my pen in my hand, the elaborate treatises of Nardini, Donatus, &c., which fill the fourth volume of the Roman Antiquities of Graevius. 2. I next undertook and finished the Italia Antiqua of Cluverius, a learned native of Prussia, who had measured, on foot, every spot, and has compiled and digested every passage of the ancient writers. These passages in Greek or Latin authors I perused in the text of Cluverius, in two folio volumes: but I separately read the descriptions of Italy by Strabo, Pliny, and Pomponius Mela, the Catalogues of the Epic poets, the Itineraries of Wesseling's Antoninus, and the coasting Voyage of Rutilius Numatianus; and I studied two kindred subjects in the Measures Itineraires of d'Anville, and the copious work of Bergier, Histoire des grands Chemins de l'Empire Romain. From these materials I formed a table of roads and distances reduced to our English measure; filled a folio common-place book with my collections and remarks on the geography of Italy; and inserted in my journal many long and learned notes on the insulae and populousness of Rome, the social war, the passage of the Alps by Hannibal, &c. 3. After glancing my eye over Addison's agreeable dialogues, I more seriously read the great work of Ezechiel Spanheim de Praestantia et Usu Numismatum, and applied with him the medals of the kings and emperors, the families and colonies, to the illustration of ancient history. And thus was I armed for my Italian journey.

I shall advance with rapid brevity in the narrative of this tour, in which somewhat more than a year (April 1764-May 1765) was agreeably employed. Content with tracing my line of march, and slightly touching on my personal feelings, I shall waive the minute investigation of the scenes which have been viewed by thousands, and described by hundreds, of our modern travellers. ROME is the great object of our pilgrimage: and 1st, the journey; 2d, the residence; and 3d, the return; will form the most proper and perspicuous division. 1. I climbed Mount Cenis, and descended into the plain of Piedmont, not on the back of an elephant, but on a light osier seat, in the hands of the dextrous and intrepid chairmen of the Alps. The architecture and government of Turin presented the same aspect of tame and tiresome uniformity: but the court was regulated with decent and splendid oeconomy; and I was introduced to his Sardinian majesty Charles Emanuel, who, after the incomparable Frederic, held the second rank (proximus longo tamen intervallo) among the kings of Europe. The size and populousness of Milan could not surprise an inhabitant of London: but the fancy is amused by a visit to the Boromean Islands, an enchanted palace, a work of the fairies in the midst of a lake encompassed with mountains, and far removed from the haunts of men. I was less amused by the marble palaces of Genoa, than by the recent memorials of her deliverance (in December 1746) from the Austrian tyranny; and I took a military survey of every scene of action within the inclosure of her double walls. My steps were detained at Parma and Modena, by the precious relics of the Farnese and Este collections: but, alas! the far greater part had been already transported, by inheritance or purchase, to Naples and Dresden. By the road of Bologna and the Apennine I at last reached Florence, where I reposed from June to September, during the heat of the summer months. In the Gallery, and especially in the Tribune, I first acknowledged, at the feet of the Venus of Medicis, that the chisel may dispute the pre-eminence with the pencil, a truth in the fine arts which cannot on this side of the Alps be felt or understood. At home I had taken some lessons of Italian on the spot I read, with a learned native, the classics of the Tuscan idiom: but the shortness of my time, and the use of the French language, prevented my acquiring any facility of speaking; and I was a silent spectator in the conversations of our envoy, Sir Horace Mann, whose most serious business was that of entertaining the English at his hospitable table. After leaving Florence, I compared the solitude of Pisa with the industry of Lucca and Leghorn, and continued my journey through Sienna to Rome, where I arrived in the beginning of October. 2. My temper is not very susceptible of enthusiasm; and the enthusiasm which I do not feel, I have ever scorned to affect. But, at the distance of twenty-five years, I can neither forget nor express the strong emotions which agitated my mind as I first approached and entered the eternal city. After a sleepless night, I trod, with a lofty step, the ruins of the Forum; each memorable spot where Romulus stood, or Tully spoke, or Caesar fell, was at once present to my eye; and several days of intoxication were lost or enjoyed before I could descend to a cool and minute investigation. My guide was Mr. Byers, a Scotch antiquary of experience and taste; but, in the daily labour of eighteen weeks, the powers of attention were sometimes fatigued, till I was myself qualified, in a last review, to select and study the capital works of ancient and modern art. Six weeks were borrowed for my tour of Naples, the most populous of cities, relative to its size, whose luxurious inhabitants seem to dwell on the confines of paradise and hell-fire. I was presented to the boy-king by our new envoy, Sir William Hamilton; who, wisely diverting his correspondence from the Secretary of State to the Royal Society and British Museum, has elucidated a country of such inestimable value to the naturalist and antiquarian. On my return, I fondly embraced, for the last time, the miracles of Rome; but I departed without kissing the feet of Rezzonico (Clement XIII.), who neither possessed the wit of his predecessor Lambertini, nor the virtues of his successor Ganganelli. 3. In my pilgrimage from Rome to Loretto I again crossed the Apennine; from the coast of the Adriatic I traversed a fruitful and populous country, which could alone disprove the paradox of Montesquieu, that modern Italy is a desert. Without adopting the exclusive prejudice of the natives, I sincerely admire the paintings of the Bologna school. I hastened to escape from the sad solitude of Ferrara, which in the age of Caesar was still more desolate. The spectacle of Venice afforded some hours of astonishment; the university of Padua is a dying taper: but Verona still boasts her amphitheatre, and his native Vicenza is adorned by the classic architecture of Palladio: the road of Lombardy and Piedmont (did Montesquieu find them without inhabitants?) led me back to Milan, Turin, and the passage of Mount Cenis, where I again crossed the Alps in my way to Lyons.

The use of foreign travel has been often debated as a general question; but the conclusion must be finally applied to the character and circumstances of each individual. With the education of boys, where or how they may pass over some juvenile years with the least mischief to themselves or others, I have no concern. But after supposing the previous and indispensable requisites of age, judgment, a competent knowledge of men and books, and a freedom from domestic prejudices, I will briefly describe the qualifications which I deem most essential to a traveller. He should be endowed with an active, indefatigable vigour of mind and body, which can seize every mode of conveyance, and support, with a careless smile, every hardship of the road, the weather, or the inn. The benefits of foreign travel will correspond with the degrees of these qualifications; but, in this sketch, those to whom I am known will not accuse me of framing my own panegyric. It was at Rome, on the 15th of October 1764, as I sat musing amidst the ruins of the Capitol, while the bare-footed fryars were singing vespers in the temple of Jupiter, that the idea of writing the decline and fall of the city first started to my mind. But my original plan was circumscribed to the decay of the city rather than of the empire: and though my reading and reflections began to point towards that object, some years elapsed, and several avocations intervened, before I was seriously engaged in the execution of that laborious work.

I had not totally renounced the southern provinces of France, but the letters which I found at Lyons were expressive of some impatience. Rome and Italy had satiated my curious appetite, and I was now ready to return to the peaceful retreat of my family and books. After a happy fortnight I reluctantly left Paris, embarked at Calais, again landed at Dover, after an interval of two years and five months, and hastily drove through the summer dust and solitude of London. On June 25 1765 I arrived at my father's house: and the five years and a half between my travels and my father's death (1770) are the portion of my life which I passed with the least enjoyment, and which I remember with the least satisfaction. Every spring I attended the monthly meeting and exercise of the militia at Southampton; and by the resignation of my father, and the death of Sir Thomas Worsley, I was successively promoted to the rank of major and lieutenant-colonel commandant; but I was each year more disgusted with the inn, the wine, the company, and the tiresome repetition of annual attendance and daily exercise. At home, the oeconomy of the family and farm still maintained the same creditable appearance. My connection with Mrs. Gibbon was mellowed into a warm and solid attachment: my growing years abolished the distance that might yet remain between a parent and a son, and my behaviour satisfied my father, who was proud of the success, however imperfect in his own life-time, of my literary talents. Our solitude was soon and often enlivened by the visit of the friend of my youth, Mr. Deyverdun, whose absence from Lausanne I had sincerely lamented. About three years after my first departure, he had emigrated from his native lake to the banks of the Oder in Germany. The res augusta domi, the waste of a decent patrimony, by an improvident father, obliged him, like many of his countrymen, to confide in his own industry; and he was entrusted with the education of a young prince, the grandson of the Margrave of Schavedt, of the Royal Family of Prussia. Our friendship was never cooled, our correspondence was sometimes interrupted; but I rather wished than hoped to obtain Mr. Deyverdun for the companion of my Italian tour. An unhappy, though honourable passion, drove him from his German court; and the attractions of hope and curiosity were fortified by the expectation of my speedy return to England. During four successive summers he passed several weeks or months at Beriton, and our free conversations, on every topic that-could interest the heart or understanding, would have reconciled me to a desert or a prison. In the winter months of London my sphere of knowledge and action was somewhat enlarged, by the many new acquaintance which I had contracted in the militia and abroad; and I must regret, as more than an acquaintance, Mr. Godfrey Clarke of Derbyshire, an amiable and worthy young man, who was snatched away by an untimely death. A weekly convivial meeting was established by myself and travellers, under the name of the Roman Club.

The renewal, or perhaps the improvement, of my English life was embittered by the alteration of my own feelings. At the age of twenty-one I was, in my proper station of a youth, delivered from the yoke of education, and delighted with the comparative state of liberty and affluence. My filial obedience was natural and easy; and in the gay prospect of futurity, my ambition did not extend beyond the enjoyment of my books, my leisure, and my patrimonial estate, undisturbed by the cares of a family and the duties of a profession. But in the militia I was armed with power; in my travels, I was exempt from controul; and as I approached, as I gradually passed my thirtieth year, I began to feel the desire of being master to my own house. The most gentle authority will sometimes frown without reason, the most cheerful submission will sometimes murmur without cause; and such is the law of our imperfect nature, that we must either command or obey; that our personal liberty is supported by the obsequiousness of our own dependants. While so many of my acquaintance were married or in parliament, or advancing with a rapid step in the various roads of honour and fortune, I stood alone, immoveable and insignificant; for after the monthly meeting of 1770, I had even withdrawn myself from the militia, by the resignation of an empty and barren commission. My temper is not susceptible of envy, and the view of successful merit has always excited my warmest applause. The miseries of a vacant life were never known to a man whose hours were insufficient for the inexhaustible pleasures of study. But I lamented that at the proper age I had not embraced the lucrative pursuits of the law or of trade, the chances of civil office or India adventure, or even the fat slumbers of the church; and my repentance became more lively as the loss of time was more irretrievable. Experience shewed me the use of grafting my private consequence on the importance of a great professional body; the benefits of those firm connections which are cemented by hope and interest, by gratitude and emulation, by the mutual exchange of services and favours. From the emoluments of a profession I might have derived an ample fortune, or a competent income, instead of being stinted to the same narrow allowance, to be increased only by an event which I sincerely deprecated. The progress and the knowledge of our domestic disorders aggravated my anxiety, and I began to apprehend that I might be left in my old age without the fruits either of industry or inheritance.

In the first summer after my return, whilst I enjoyed at Beriton the society of my friend Deyverdun, our daily conversations expatiated over the field of ancient and modern literature; and we freely discussed my studies, my first Essay, and my future projects. The Decline and Fall of Rome I still contemplated at an awful distance: but the two historical designs which had balanced my choice were submitted to his taste: and in the parallel between the Revolutions of Florence and Switzerland, our common partiality for a country which was his by birth, and mine by adoption, inclined the scale in favour of the latter. According to the plan, which was soon conceived and digested, I embraced a period of two hundred years, from the association of the three peasants of the Alps to the plenitude and prosperity of the Helvetic body in the sixteenth century. I should have described the deliverance and victory of the Swiss, who have never shed the blood of their tyrants but in a field of battle; the laws and manners of the confederate states; the splendid trophies of the Austrian, Burgundian, and Italian wars; and the wisdom of a nation, which, after some sallies of martial adventure, has been content to guard the blessings of peace with the sword of freedom.

—Manus haec inimica tyrannis
Ense petit placidam sub libertate quietem.

My judgment, as well as my enthusiasm, was satisfied with the glorious theme; and the assistance of Deyverdun seemed to remove an insuperable obstacle. The French or Latin memorials, of which I was not ignorant, are inconsiderable in number and weight; but in the perfect acquaintance of my friend with the German language, I found the key of a more valuable collection. The most necessary books were procured; he translated, for my use, the folio volume of Schilling, a copious and contemporary relation of the war of Burgundy; we read and marked the most interesting parts of the great chronicle of Tschudi; and by his labour, or that of an inferior assistant, large extracts were made from the History of Lauffer and the Dictionary of Lew: yet such was the distance and delay, that two years elapsed in these preparatory steps; and it was late in the third summer (1767) before I entered, with these slender materials, on the more agreeable task of composition. A specimen of my History, the first book, was read the following winter in a literary society of foreigners in London; and as the author was unknown, I listened, without observation, to the free strictures, and unfavourable sentence, of my judges. The momentary sensation was painful; but their condemnation was ratified by my cooler thoughts. I delivered my imperfect sheets to the flames,—and for ever renounced a design in which some expence, much labour, and more time had been so vainly consumed. I cannot regret the loss of a slight and superficial essay, for such the work must have been in the hands of a stranger, uninformed by the scholars and statesmen, and remote from the libraries and archives of the Swiss republics. My ancient habits, and the presence of Deyverdun, encouraged me to write in French for the continent of Europe; but I was conscious myself that my style, above prose and below poetry, degenerated into a verbose and turgid declamation. Perhaps I may impute the failure to the injudicious choice of a foreign language. Perhaps I may suspect that the language itself is ill adapted to sustain the vigour and dignity of an important narrative. But if France, so rich in literary merit, had produced a great original historian, his genius would have formed and fixed the idiom to the proper tone, the peculiar model of historical eloquence.

It was in search of some liberal and lucrative employment that my friend Deyverdun had visited England. His remittances from home were scanty and precarious. My purse was always open, but it was often empty; and I bitterly felt the want of riches and power, which might have enabled me to correct the errors of his fortune. His wishes and qualifications solicited the station of the travelling governor of some wealthy pupil; but every vacancy provoked so many eager candidates, that for a long time I struggled without success; nor was it till after much application that I could even place him as a clerk in the office of the secretary of state. In a residence of several years he never acquired the just pronunciation and familiar use of the English tongue, but he read our most difficult authors with ease and taste: his critical knowledge of our language and poetry was such as few foreigners have possessed; and few of our countrymen could enjoy the theatre of Shakspeare and Garrick with more exquisite feeling and discernment. The consciousness of his own strength, and the assurance of my aid, emboldened him to imitate the example of Dr. Maty, whose Journal Britannique was esteemed and regretted; and to improve his model, by uniting with the transactions of literature a philosophic view of the arts and manners of the British nation. Our journal for the year 1767, under the title of Memoires Literaires de la Grand Bretagne, was soon finished, and sent to the press. For the first article, Lord Lyttelton's History of Henry II., I must own myself responsible; but the public has ratified my judgment of that voluminous work, in which sense and learning are not illuminated by a ray of genius. The next specimen was the choice of my friend, the Bath Guide, a light and whimsical performance, of local, and even verbal, pleasantry. I started at the attempt: he smiled at my fears: his courage was justified by success; and a master of both languages will applaud the curious felicity with which he has transfused into French prose the spirit, and even the humour, of the English verse. It is not my wish to deny how deeply I was interested in these Memoirs, of which I need not surely be ashamed; but at the distance of more than twenty years, it would be impossible for me to ascertain the respective shares of the two associates. A long and intimate communication of ideas had cast our sentiments and style in the same mould. In our social labours we composed and corrected by turns; and the praise which I might honestly bestow, would fall perhaps on some article or passage most properly my own. A second volume (for the year 1768) was published of these Memoirs. I will presume to say, that their merit was superior to their reputation; but it is not less true, that they were productive of more reputation than emolument. They introduced my friend to the protection, and myself to the acquaintance, of the Earl of Chesterfield, whose age and infirmities secluded him from the world; and of Mr. David Hume, who was under-secretary to the office in which Deyverdun was more humbly employed. The former accepted a dedication,(April 12, 1769,) and reserved the author for the future education of his successor: the latter enriched the Journal with a reply to Mr. Walpole's Historical Doubts, which he afterwards shaped into the form of a note. The materials of the third volume were almost completed, when I recommended Deyverdun as governor to Sir Richard Worsley, a youth, the son of my old Lieutenant-colonel, who was lately deceased. They set forwards on their travels; nor did they return to England till some time after my father's death.

My next publication was an accidental sally of love and resentment; of my reverence for modest genius, and my aversion for insolent pedantry. The sixth book of the AEneid is the most pleasing and perfect composition of Latin poetry. The descent of AEneas and the Sibyl to the infernal regions, to the world of spirits, expands an awful and boundless prospect, from the nocturnal gloom of the Cumaean grot,

> Ibant obscuri sola sub nocte per umbram,

to the meridian brightness of the Elysian fields;

> Largior hic campos aether et lumine vestit
> Purpureo—

from the dreams of simple Nature, to the dreams, alas! of Egyptian theology, and the philosophy of the Greeks. But the final dismission of the hero through the ivory gate, whence

> Falsa ad coelum mittunt insomnia manes,

seems to dissolve the whole enchantment, and leaves the reader in a state of cold and anxious scepticism. This most lame and impotent conclusion has been variously imputed to the taste or irreligion of Virgil; but, according to the more elaborate interpretation of

Bishop Warburton, the descent to hell is not a false, but a mimic scene; which represents the initiation of AEneas, in the character of a law-giver, to the Eleusinian mysteries. This hypothesis, a singular chapter in the Divine Legation of Moses, had been admitted by many as true; it was praised by all as ingenious; nor had it been exposed, in a space of thirty years, to a fair and critical discussion. The learning and the abilities of the author had raised him to a just eminence; but he reigned the dictator and tyrant of the world of literature. The real merit of Warburton was degraded by the pride and presumption with which he pronounced his infallible decrees; in his polemic writings he lashed his antagonists without mercy or moderation; and his servile flatterers, (see the base and malignant Essay on the Delicacy of Friendship,) exalting the master critic far above Aristotle and Longinus, assaulted every modest dissenter who refused to consult the oracle, and to adore the idol. In a land of liberty, such despotism must provoke a general opposition, and the zeal of opposition is seldom candid or impartial. A late professor of Oxford, (Dr. Lowth,) in a pointed and polished epistle, (Aug. 31, 1765,) defended himself, and attacked the Bishop; and, whatsoever might be the merits of an insignificant controversy, his victory was clearly established by the silent confusion of Warburton and his slaves. I too, without any private offence, was ambitious of breaking a lance against the giant's shield; and in the beginning of the year 1770, my Critical Observations on the Sixth Book of the AEneid were sent, without my name, to the press. In this short Essay, my first English publication, I aimed my strokes against the person and the hypothesis of Bishop Warburton. I proved, at least to my own satisfaction, that the ancient lawgivers did not invent the mysteries, and that AEneas was never invested with the office of lawgiver: that there is not any argument, any circumstance, which can melt a fable into allegory, or remove the scene from the Lake Avernus to the Temple of Ceres: that such a wild supposition is equally injurious to the poet and the man: that if Virgil was not initiated he could not, if he were, he would not, reveal the secrets of the initiation: that the anathema of Horace (vetabo qui Cereris sacrum vulgarit, &c.) at once attests his own ignorance and the innocence of his friend. As the Bishop of Gloucester and his party maintained a discreet silence, my critical disquisition was soon lost among the pamphlets of the day; but the public coldness was overbalanced to my feelings by the weighty approbation of the last and best editor of Virgil, Professor Heyne of Gottingen, who acquiesces in my confutation, and styles the unknown author, doctus — et elegantissimus Britannus. But I cannot resist the temptation of transcribing the favourable judgment of Mr. Hayley, himself a poet and a scholar "An intricate hypothesis, twisted into a long and laboured chain of quotation and argument, the Dissertation on the Sixth Book of Virgil, remained some time unrefuted. — At length, a superior, but anonymous, critic arose, who, in one of the most judicious and spirited essays that our nation has produced, on a point of classical literature, completely overturned this ill-founded edifice, and exposed the arrogance and futility of its assuming architect." He even condescends to justify an acrimony of style, which had been gently blamed by the more unbiassed German; "Paullo acrius quam velis — perstrinxit." But I cannot forgive myself the contemptuous treatment of a span who, with all his faults, was entitled to my esteem; [Note: The Divine Legation of Moses is a monument, already crumbling in the dust, of the vigour and weakness of the human mind. If Warburton's new argument proved anything, it would be a demonstration against the legislator, who left his people without the knowledge of a future state. But some episodes of the work, on the Greek philosophy, the hieroglyphics of Egypt, &c. are entitled to the praise of learning, imagination, and discernment.] and I can less forgive, in a personal attack, the cowardly concealment of my name and character.

In the fifteen years between my Essay on the Study of Literature and the first volume of the Decline and Fall, (1761-1776,) this criticism on Warburton, and some articles in the journal, were my sole publications. It is more especially incumbent on me to mark the employment, or to confess the waste of time, from my travels to my father's death, an interval in which I was not diverted by any professional duties from the labours and pleasures of a studious life. 1. As soon as I was released from the fruitless task of the Swiss revolutions, (1768,) I began gradually to advance from the wish to the hope, from the hope to the design, from the design to the execution, of my historical work, of whose limits and extent I had yet a very inadequate notion. The Classics, as low as Tacitus, the younger Pliny, and Juvenal, were my old and familiar companions. I insensibly plunged into the ocean of the Augustan history; and in the descending series I investigated, with my pen almost always in my hand, the original records, both Greek and Latin, from Dion Cassius to Ammianus Marcellinus, from the reign of Trajan to the last age of the Western Caesars. The subsidiary rays of medals, and inscriptions of geography and chronology, were thrown on their proper objects; and I applied the collections of Tillemont, whose inimitable accuracy almost assumes the character of genius, to fix and arrange within my reach the loose and scattered atoms of historical information. Through the darkness of the middle ages I explored my way in the Annals and Antiquities of Italy of the learned Muratori; and diligently compared them with the parallel or transverse lines of Sigonius and Maffei, Baronius and Pagi, till I almost grasped the ruins of Rome in the fourteenth century, without suspecting that this final chapter must be attained by the labour of six quartos and twenty years. Among the books which I purchased, the Theodocian Code, with the commentary of James Godefroy, must be gratefully remembered. I used it (and much I used it) as a work of history, rather than of jurisprudence: but in every light it may be considered as a full and capacious repository of the political state of the empire in the fourth and fifth centuries. As I believed, and as I still believe, that the propagation of the Gospel, and the triumph of the church, are inseparably connected with the decline of the Roman monarchy, I weighed the causes and effects of the revolution, and contrasted the narratives and apologies of the Christians themselves, with the glances of candour or enmity which the Pagans have cast on the rising sects, The Jewish and Heathen testimonies, as they are collected and illustrated by Dr. Lardner, directed, without superseding, my search of the originals; and in an ample dissertation on the miraculous darkness of the passion, I privately withdrew my conclusions from the silence of an unbelieving age. I have assembled the preparatory studies, directly or indirectly relative to my history; but, in strict equity, they must be spread beyond this period of my life, over the two summers (1771 and 1772) that elapsed between my father's death and my settlement in London. 2. In a free conversation with books and men, it would be endless to enumerate the names and characters of all who are introduced to our acquaintance; but in this general acquaintance we may select the degrees of friendship and esteem, according to the wise maxim, Multum legere potius quam multa. I reviewed, again and again, the immortal works of the French and English, the Latin and Italian classics. My Greek studies (though less assiduous than I designed) maintained and extended my knowledge of that incomparable idiom. Homer and Xenophon were still my favourite authors; and I had almost prepared for the press an Essay on the Cyropoedia, which, in my own judgment, is not unhappily laboured. After a certain age, the new publications of merit are the sole food of the many; and the must austere student will be often tempted to break the line, for the sake of indulging his own curiosity, and of providing the topics of fashionable currency. A more respectable motive maybe assigned for the third perusal of Blackstone's Commentaries, and a copious and critical abstract of that English work was my first serious production in my native language. 3. My literary leisure was much less complete and independent than it might appear to the eye of a stranger. In the hurry of London I was destitute of books; in the solitude of Hampshire I was not master of my time. My quiet was gradually disturbed by our domestic anxiety, and I should be ashamed of my unfeeling philosophy, had I found much time or taste for study in the last fatal summer (1770) of my father's decay and dissolution.

The disembodying of the militia at the close of the war (1763) had restored the Major (a new Cincinnatus) to a life of agriculture. His labours were useful, his pleasures innocent, his wishes moderate; and my father seemed to enjoy the state of happiness which is celebrated by poets and philosophers, as the most agreeable to nature, and the least accessible to fortune.

> Beatus ille, qui procul negotiis
> (Ut prisca gens mortalium)
> Paterna rura bubus exercet suis,
> Solutus omni foenore.
> > HOR. Epod. ii.

> Like the first mortals, blest is he,
> From debts, and usury, and business free,
> With his own team who ploughs the soil,
> Which grateful once confessed his father's toil.
> > FRANCIS.

But the last indispensable condition, the freedom from debt, was wanting to my father's felicity; and the vanities of his youth were severely punished by the solicitude and sorrow of his declining age. The first mortgage, on my return from Lausanne, (1758,) had afforded him a partial and transient relief. The annual demand of interest and allowance was a heavy deduction from his income; the militia was a source of expence, the farm in his hands was not a profitable adventure, he was loaded with the costs and damages of an obsolete law-suit; and each year multiplied the number, and exhausted the patience, of his creditors. Under these painful circumstances, I consented to an additional mortgage, to the sale of Putney, and to every sacrifice that could alleviate his distress. But he was no longer capable of a rational effort, and his reluctant delays postponed not the evils themselves, but the remedies of those evils (remedia malorum potius quam mala differebat). The pangs of shame, tenderness, and self-reproach, incessantly preyed on his vitals; his constitution was broken; he lost his strength and his sight; the rapid progress of a dropsy admonished him of his end, and he sunk into the grave on Nov. 10, 1770, in the sixty-fourth year of his age. A family tradition insinuates that Mr. William Law had drawn his pupil in the light and inconstant character of Flatus, who is ever confident, and ever disappointed in the chace of happiness. But these constitutional failing were happily compensated by the virtues of the head and heart, by the warmest sentiments of honour and humanity. His graceful person, polite address, gentle manners, and unaffected cheerfulness, recommended him to the favour of every company; and in the change of times and opinions, his liberal spirit had long since delivered him from the zeal and prejudice of a Tory education. I submitted to the order of Nature; and my grief was soothed by the conscious satisfaction that I had discharged all the duties of filial piety.

As soon as I had paid the last solemn duties to my father, and obtained, from time and reason, a tolerable composure of mind, I began to form the plan of an independent life, most adapted to my circumstances and inclination. Yet so intricate was the net, my efforts were so awkward and feeble, that nearly two years (Nov. 1770-Oct. 1772) were suffered to elapse before I could disentangle myself from the management of the farm, and transfer my residence from Beriton to a house in London. During this interval I continued to divide my year between town and the country; but my new situation was brightened by hope; my stay in London was prolonged into the summer; and the uniformity of the summer was occasionally broken by visits and excursions at a distance from home. The gratification of my desires (they were not immoderate) has been seldom disappointed by the want of money or credit; my pride was never insulted by the visit of an importunate tradesman; and my transient anxiety for the past or future has been dispelled by the studious or social occupation of the present hour. My conscience does not accuse me of any act of extravagance or injustice, and the remnant of my estate affords an ample and honourable provision for my declining age. I shall not expatiate on my oeconomical affairs, which cannot be instructive or amusing to the reader. It is a rule of prudence, as well as of politeness, to reserve such confidence for the ear of a private friend, without exposing our situation to the envy or pity of strangers; for envy is productive of hatred, and pity borders too nearly on contempt. Yet I may believe, and even assert, that in circumstances more indigent or more wealthy, I should never have accomplished the task, or acquired the fame, of an historian; that my spirit would have been broken by poverty and contempt, and that my industry might have been relaxed in the labour and luxury of a superfluous fortune.

I had now attained the first of earthly blessings, independence: I was the absolute master of my hours and actions: nor was I deceived in the hope that the establishment of my library in town would allow me to divide the day between study and society. Each year the circle of my acquaintance, the number of my dead and living companions, was enlarged. To a lover of books, the shops and sales of London present irresistible temptations; and the manufacture of my history required a various and growing stock of materials. The militia, my travels, the House of Commons, the fame of an author, contributed to multiply my connections: I was chosen a member of the fashionable clubs; and, before I left England in 1783, there were few persons of any eminence in the literary or political world to whom I was a stranger. [Note: From the mixed, though polite, company of Boodle's, White's, and Brooks's, I must honourably distinguish a weekly society, which was instituted in the year 1764, and which still continues to flourish, under the title of the Literary Club. (Hawkins's Life of Johnson, p.415. Boswell's

Tour to the Hebrides, p 97.) The names of Dr. Johnson, Mr. Burke, Mr. Topham Beauclerc, Mr. Garrick, Dr. Goldsmith, Sir Joshua Reynolds, Mr. Colman, Sir William Jones, Dr. Percy, Mr. Fox, Mr. Sheridan, Mr. Adam Smith, Mr. Steevens, Mr. Dunning, Sir Joseph Banks, Dr. Warton, and his brother Mr. Thomas Warton, Dr. Burney, &c., form a large and luminous constellation of British stars.] It would most assuredly be in my power to amuse the reader with a gallery of portraits and a collection of anecdotes. But I have always condemned the practice of transforming a private memorial into a vehicle of satire or praise. By my own choice I passed in town the greatest part of the year; but whenever I was desirous of breathing the air of the country, I possessed an hospitable retreat at Sheffield-place in Sussex, in the family of my valuable friend Mr. Holroyd, whose character, under the name of Lord Sheffield, has since been more conspicuous to the public.

No sooner was I settled in my house and library, than I undertook the composition of the first volume of my History. At the outset all was dark and doubtful; even the title of the work, the true aera of the Decline and Fall of the Empire, the limits of the introduction, the division of the chapters, and the order of the narrative; and I was often tempted to cast away the labour of seven years. The style of an author should be the image of his mind, but the choice and command of language is the fruit of exercise. Many experiments were made before I could hit the middle tone between a dull chronicle and a rhetorical declamation: three times did I compose the first chapter, and twice the second and third, before I was tolerably satisfied with their effect. In the remainder of the way I advanced with a more equal and easy pace; but the fifteenth and sixteenth chapters have been reduced by three successive revisals, from a large volume to their present size; and they might still be compressed, without any loss of facts or sentiments. An opposite fault may be imputed to the concise and superficial narrative of the first reigns from Commodus to Alexander; a fault of which I have never heard, except from Mr. Hume in his last journey to London. Such an oracle might have been consulted and obeyed with rational devotion; but I was soon disgusted with the modest practice of reading the manuscript to my friends. Of such friends some will praise from politeness, and some will criticise from vanity. The author himself is the best judge of his own performance; no one has so deeply meditated on the subject; no one is so sincerely interested in the event.

By the friendship of Mr. (now Lord) Eliot, who had married my first cousin, I was returned at the general election for the borough of Liskeard. I took my seat at the beginning of the memorable contest between Great Britain and America, and supported, with many a sincere and silent vote, the rights, though not, perhaps, the interest, of the mother country. After a fleeting illusive hope, prudence condemned me to acquiesce in the humble station of a mute. I was not armed by Nature and education with the intrepid energy of mind and voice.

Vincentem strepitus, et natum rebus agendis.

Timidity was fortified by pride, and even the success of my pen discouraged the trial of my voice. But I assisted at the debates of a free assembly; I listened to the attack and defence of eloquence and reason; I had a near prospect of the characters, views, and passions of the first men of the age. The cause of government was ably vindicated by Lord North, a statesman of spotless integrity, a consummate master of debate, who could wield, with equal dexterity, the arms of reason and of ridicule. He was seated on the Treasury-bench between his Attorney and Solicitor General, the two pillars of the law and state, magis pares quam similes; and the minister might indulge in a short slumber, whilst he was upholden on either hand by the majestic sense of Thurlow, and the skilful eloquence of Wedderburne. From the adverse side of the house an ardent and powerful opposition was supported, by the lively declamation of Barre, the legal acuteness of Dunning, the profuse and philosophic fancy of Burke, and the argumentative vehemence of Fox, who in the conduct of a party approved himself equal to the conduct of an empire. By such men every operation of peace and war, every principle of justice or policy, every question of authority and freedom, was attacked and defended; and the subject of the momentous contest was the union or separation of Great Britain and America. The eight sessions that I sat in parliament were a school of civil prudence, the first and most essential virtue of an historian.

The volume of my History, which had been somewhat delayed by the novelty and tumult of a first session, was now ready for the press. After the perilous adventure had been declined by my friend Mr. Elmsly, I agreed, upon easy terms, with Mr. Thomas Cadell, a respectable bookseller, and Mr. William Strahan, an eminent printer; and they undertook the care and risk of the publication, which derived more credit from the name of the shop than from that of the author. The last revisal of the proofs was submitted to my vigilance; and many blemishes of style, which had been invisible in the manuscript, were discovered and corrected in the printed sheet. So moderate were our hopes, that the original impression had been stinted to five hundred, till the number was doubled by the prophetic taste of Mr. Strahan. During this awful interval I was neither elated by the ambition of fame, nor depressed by the apprehension of contempt. My diligence and accuracy were attested by my own conscience. History is the most popular species of writing, since it can adapt itself to the highest or the lowest capacity. I had chosen an illustrious subject. Rome is familiar to the school-boy and the statesman; and my narrative was deduced from the last period of classical reading. I had likewise flattered myself, that an age of light and liberty would receive, without scandal, an inquiry into the human causes of the progress and establishment of Christianity.

I am at a loss how to describe the success of the work, without betraying the vanity of the writer. The first impression was exhausted in a few days; a second and third edition were scarcely adequate to the demand; and the bookseller's property was twice invaded by the pirates of Dublin. My book was on every table, and almost on every toilette; the historian was crowned by the taste or fashion of the day; nor was the general voice disturbed by the barking of any profane critic. The favour of mankind is most freely bestowed on a new acquaintance of any original merit; and the mutual surprise of the public and their favourite is productive of those warm sensibilities, which at a second meeting can no longer be rekindled. If I listened to the music of praise, I was more seriously satisfied with the approbation of my judges. The candour of Dr. Robertson embraced his disciple. A letter from Mr. Hume overpaid the labour of ten years, but I have never presumed to accept a place in the triumvirate of British historians.

That curious and original letter will amuse the reader, and his gratitude should shield my free communication from the reproach of vanity.

"DEAR SIR, EDINBURGH, 18th March 1776.

"As I ran through your volume of history with great avidity and impatience, I cannot forbear discovering somewhat of the same impatience in returning you thanks for your agreeable present, and expressing the satisfaction which the performance has given me. Whether I consider the dignity of your style, the depth of your matter, or the extensiveness of your learning, I must regard the work as equally the object of esteem; and I own that if I had not previously had the happiness of your personal acquaintance, such a performance from an Englishman in our age would have given me some surprise. You may smile at this sentiment; but as it seems to me that your countrymen, for almost a whole generation, have given themselves up to barbarous and absurd faction, and have totally neglected all polite letters, I no longer expected any valuable production ever to come from them. I know it will give you pleasure (as it did me) to find that all the men of letters in this place concur in the admiration of your work, and in their anxious desire of your continuing it.

"When I heard of your undertaking, (which was some time ago,) I own I was a little curious to see how you would extricate yourself from the subject of your two last chapters. I think you have observed a very prudent temperament; but it was impossible to treat the subject so as not to give grounds of suspicion against you, and you may expect that a clamour will arise. This, if anything, will retard your success with the public; for in every other respect your work is calculated to be popular. But among many other marks of decline, the prevalence of superstition in England prognosticates the fall of philosophy and decay of taste; and though nobody be more capable than you to revive them, you will probably find a struggle in your first advances.

"I see you entertain a great doubt with regard to the authenticity of the poems of Ossian. You are certainly right in so doing. It is indeed strange that any men of sense could have imagined it possible, that above twenty thousand verses, along with numberless historical facts, could have been preserved by oral tradition during fifty generations, by the rudest, perhaps, of all the European nations, the most necessitous, the most turbulent, and the most unsettled. Where a supposition is so contrary to common sense, any positive evidence of it ought never to be regarded. Men run with great avidity to give their evidence in favour of what flatters their passions and their national prejudices. You are therefore over and above indulgent to us in speaking of the matter with hesitation.

"I must inform you that we all are very anxious to hear that you have fully collected the materials for your second volume, and that you are even considerably advanced in the composition of it. I speak this more in the name of my friends than in my own; as I cannot expect to live so long as to see the publication of it. Your ensuing volume will be more delicate than the preceding, but I trust in your prudence for extricating you from the difficulties; and, in all events, you have courage to despise the clamour of bigots.

I am, with great regard,
Dear Sir, &c. DAVID HUME."

Some weeks afterwards I had the melancholy pleasure of seeing Mr. Hume in his passage through London; his body feeble, his mind firm. On Aug. 25 of the same year (1776) he died, at Edinburgh, the death of a philosopher.

My second excursion to Paris was determined by the pressing invitation of M. and Madame Necker, who had visited England in the preceding summer. On my arrival I found M. Necker Director-general of the finances, in the first bloom of power and popularity. His private fortune enabled him to support a liberal establishment, and his wife, whose talents and virtues I had long admired, was admirably qualified to preside in the conversation of her table and drawing-room. As their friend, I was introduced to the best company of both sexes; to the foreign ministers of all nations, and to the first names and characters of France; who distinguished me by such marks of civility and kindness, as gratitude will not suffer me to forget, and modesty will not allow me to enumerate.

The fashionable suppers often broke into the morning hours; yet I occasionally consulted the Royal Library, and that of the Abbey of St. Germain, and in the free use of their books at home I had always reason to praise the liberality of those institutions. The society of men of letters I neither courted nor declined; but I was happy in the acquaintance of M. de Buffon, who united with a sublime genius the most amiable simplicity of mind and manners. At the table of my old friend, M. de Foncemagne, I was involved in a dispute with the Abbe de Mably; and his jealous irascible spirit revenged itself on a work which he was incapable of reading in the original.

As I might be partial in my own cause, I shall transcribe the words of an unknown critic, observing only, that this dispute had been preceded by another on the English constitution, at the house of the Countess de Froulay, an old Jansenist lady.

"Vous etiez chez M. de Foncemagne, mon cher Theodon, le jour que M. l'Abbe de Mably et M. Gibbon y dinerent en grande compagnie. La conversation roula presque entierement sur l'histoire. L'Abbe etant un profond politique, la tourna sur l'administration, quand on fut au desert: et comme par caractere, par humeur, par l'habitude d'admirer Tite Live, il ne prise que le systeme republicain, il se mit a vanter l'excellence des republiques; bien persuade que le savant Anglois l'approuveroit en tout, et admireroit la profondeur de genie qui avoit fait deviner tous ces avantages a un Francois. Mais M. Gibbon, instruit par l'experience des inconveniens d'un gouvernement populaire, ne fut point du tout de son avis, et il prit genereusement la defense du gouvernement monarchique. L'Abbe voulut le convaincre par Tite Live, et par quelques argumens tires de Plutarque en faveur des Spartiates. M. Gibbon, doue de la memoire la plus heureuse, et ayant tous les faits presens a la pensee, domina bien-tot la conversation; l'Abbe se facha, il s'emporta, il dit des choses dures; l'Anglois, conservant le phlegme de son pays, prenoit ses avantages, et pressoit l'Abbe avec d'autant plus de succes que la colere le troubloit de plus en plus. La conversation s'echauffoit, et M. de Foncemagne la rompit en se levant de table, et en passant dans le salon, ou personne ne fut tente de la renouer."—Supplement de la Maniere d'ecrire l'Histoire, p. 125, &c. [Note: Of the voluminous writings of the Abbe de Mably, (see his Eloge by the Abbe Brizard,) the Principes du droit public de l'Europe, and the first part of the Observ. sur l'Hist. de France, may be deservedly praised; and even the Maniere d'ecrire l'Hist. contains several useful precepts and judicious remarks. Mably was a lover of virtue and freedom; but his virtue was austere, and his freedom was impatient of an equal. Kings, magistrates, nobles, and successful writers were the objects of his contempt, or hatred, or envy; but his illiberal abuse of Voltaire, Hume, Buffon, the Abbe Reynal, Dr. Robertson, and tutti quanti can be injurious only to himself.]

Nearly two years had elapsed between the publication of my first and the commencement of my second volume; and the causes must be assigned of this long delay. 1. After a short holiday, I indulged my curiosity in some studies of a very different nature, a course of anatomy, which was demonstrated by Doctor Hunter; and some lessons of chymistry, which were delivered by Mr. Higgins. The principles of these sciences, and a taste for books of natural history, contributed to multiply my ideas and images; and the anatomist and chymist may sometimes track me in their own snow. 2. I dived, perhaps too deeply, into the mud of the Arian controversy; and many days of reading, thinking, and writing were consumed in the pursuit of a phantom. 3. It is difficult to arrange, with order and perspicuity, the various transactions of the age of Constantine; and so much was I displeased with the first essay, that I committed to the flames above fifty sheets. 4. The six months of Paris and pleasure must be deducted from the account. But when I resumed my task I felt my improvement; I was now master of my style and subject, and while the measure of my daily performance was enlarged, I discovered less reason to cancel or correct. It has always been my practice to cast a long paragraph in a single mould, to try it by my ear, to deposit it in my memory, but to suspend the action of the pen till I had given the last polish to my work. Shall I add, that I never found my mind more vigorous, not my composition more happy, than in the winter hurry of society and parliament?

Had I believed that the majority of English readers were so fondly attached even to the name and shadow of Christianity; had I foreseen that the pious, the timid, and the prudent, would feel, or affect to feel, with such exquisite sensibility; I might, perhaps, have softened the two invidious chapters, which would create many enemies, and conciliate few friends. But the shaft was shot, the alarm was sounded, and I could only rejoice, that if the voice of our priests was clamorous and bitter, their hands were disarmed from the powers of persecution. I adhered to the wise resolution of trusting myself and my writings to the candour of the public, till Mr. Davies of Oxford presumed to attack, not the faith, but the fidelity, of the historian. My Vindication, expressive of less anger than contempt, amused for a moment the busy and idle metropolis; and the most rational part of the laity, and even of the clergy, appear to have been satisfied of my innocence and accuracy. I would not print this Vindication in quarto, lest it should be bound and preserved with the history itself. At the distance of twelve years, I calmly affirm my judgment of Davies, Chelsum, &c. A victory over such antagonists was a sufficient humiliation. They, however, were rewarded in this world. Poor Chelsum was indeed neglected; and I dare not boast the making Dr. Watson a bishop; he is a prelate of a large mind and liberal spirit: but I enjoyed the pleasure of giving a Royal pension to Mr. Davies, and of collating Dr. Apthorpe to an archiepiscopal living. Their success encouraged the zeal of Taylor the Arian, [Note: The stupendous title, Thoughts on the Causes of the grand Apostacy, at first agitated my nerves, till I discovered that it was the apostacy of the whole church, since the Council of Nice, from Mr. Taylor's private religion. His book is a thorough mixture of high enthusiasm and low buffoonery, and the Millennium is a fundamental article of his creed.] and Milner the Methodist, [Note: From his grammar-school at Kingston upon Hull, Mr. Joseph Milner pronounces an anathema against all rational religion. His faith is a divine taste, a spiritual inspiration; his church is a mystic and invisible body: the natural Christians, such as Mr. Locke, who believe and interpret the Scriptures, are, in his judgment, no better than profane infidels.] with many others, whom it would be difficult to remember, and tedious to rehearse. The list of my adversaries, however, was graced with the more respectable names of Dr. Priestley, Sir David Dalrymple, and Dr. White; and every polemic, of either university, discharged his sermon or pamphlet against the impenetrable silence of the Roman historian. In his History of the Corruptions of Christianity, Dr. Priestley threw down his two gauntlets to Bishop Hurd and Mr. Gibbon. I declined the challenge in a letter, exhorting my opponent to enlighten the world by his philosophical discoveries, and to remember that the merit of his predecessor Servetus is now reduced to a single passage, which indicates the smaller circulation of the blood through the lungs, from and to the heart. Instead of listening to this friendly advice, the dauntless philosopher of Birmingham continued to fire away his double battery against those who believed too little, and those who believed too much. From my replies he has nothing to hope or fear: but his Socinian shield has repeatedly been pierced by the spear of Horsley, and his trumpet of sedition may at length awaken the magistrates of a free country. The profession and rank of Sir David Dalrymple (now a Lord of Session) has given a more decent colour to his style. But he scrutinized each separate passage of the two chapters with the dry minuteness of a special pleader; and as he was always solicitous to make, he may have succeeded sometimes in finding, a flaw. In his Annals of Scotland, he has shewn himself a diligent collector and an accurate critic. I have praised, and I still praise, the eloquent sermons which were preached in St. Mary's pulpit at Oxford by Dr. White. If he assaulted me with some degree of illiberal acrimony, in such a place, and before such an audience, he was obliged to speak the language of the country. I smiled at a passage in one of his private letters to Mr. Badcock; "The part where we encounter Gibbon must be brilliant and striking." In a sermon preached before the university of Cambridge, Dr. Edwards complimented a work, "which can only perish with the language itself;" and esteems the author a formidable enemy. He is, indeed, astonished that more learning and ingenuity has not been shewn in the defence of Israel; that the prelates and dignitaries of the church (alas, good man!) did not vie with each other, whose stone should sink the deepest in the forehead of this Goliath.

"But the force of truth will oblige us to confess, that in the attacks which have been levelled against our sceptical historian, we can discover but slender traces of profound and exquisite erudition, of solid criticism and accurate investigation; but we are too frequently disgusted by vague and inconclusive reasoning; by unseasonable banter and senseless witticisms; by imbittered bigotry and enthusiastic jargon; by futile cavils and illiberal invectives. Proud and elated by the weakness of his antagonists, he condescends not to handle the sword of controversy."—Monthly Review, Oct. 1790.

Let me frankly own that I was startled at the first discharge of ecclesiastical ordnance; but as soon as I found that this empty noise was mischievous only in the intention, my fear was converted into indignation; and every feeling of indignation or curiosity has long since subsided in pure and placid indifference.

The prosecution of my history was soon afterwards checked by another controversy of a very different kind. At the request of the Lord Chancellor, and of Lord Weymouth, then Secretary of State, I vindicated, against the French manifesto, the justice of the British arms. The whole correspondence of Lord Stormont, our late ambassador at Paris, was submitted to my inspection, and the Memoire Justificatif, which I composed in French, was first approved by the Cabinet Ministers, and then delivered as a State paper to the courts of Europe. The style and manner are praised by Beaumarchais himself, who, in his private quarrel, attempted a reply; but he flatters me, by ascribing the memoir to Lord Stormont; and the grossness of his invective betrays the loss of temper and of wit; he acknowledged, Oeuv. de Beaumarchais, iii. 299, 355, that le style ne seroit pas sans grace, ni la logique sans justesse, &c. if the facts were true which he undertakes to disprove. For these facts my credit is not pledged; I spoke as a lawyer from my brief, but the veracity of Beaumarchais may be estimated from the assertion that France, by the treaty of Paris (1763) was limited to a certain number of ships of war. On the application of the Duke of Choiseul, he was obliged to retract this daring falsehood.

Among the honourable connections which I had formed, I may justly be proud of the friendship of Mr. Wedderburne, at that time Attorney- General, who now illustrates the title of Lord Loughborough, and the office of Chief Justice of the Common Pleas. By his strong recommendation, and the favourable disposition of Lord North, I was appointed one of the Lords Commissioners of Trade and Plantations; and my private income was enlarged by a clear addition of between seven and eight hundred pounds a-year. The fancy of an hostile orator may paint, in the strong colours of ridicule, "the perpetual virtual adjournment, and the unbroken sitting vacation of the Board of Trade." [Note: I can never forget the delight with which that diffusive and ingenious orator, Mr. Burke, was heard by all sides of the house, and even by those whose existence he proscribed. (Speech on the Bill of Reform, p.

72-80.) The Lords of Trade blushed at their insignificancy, and Mr. Eden's appeal to the 2,500 volumes of our Reports, served only to excite a general laugh. I take this opportunity of certifying the correctness of Mr. Burke's printed speeches, which I have heard and read.] But it must be allowed that our duty was not intolerably severe, and that I enjoyed many days and weeks of repose, without being called away from my library to the office. My acceptance of a place provoked some of the leaders of opposition, with whom I had lived in habits of intimacy; and I was most unjustly accused of deserting a party, in which I had never enlisted.

The aspect of the next session of parliament was stormy and perilous; county meetings, petitions, and committees of correspondence, announced the public discontent; and instead of voting with a triumphant majority, the friends of government were often exposed to a struggle, and sometimes to a defeat. The House of Commons adopted Mr. Dunning's motion, "That the influence of the Crown had increased, was increasing, and ought to be diminished:" and Mr. Burke's bill of reform was framed with skill, introduced with eloquence, and supported by numbers. Our late president, the American Secretary of State, very narrowly escaped the sentence of proscription; but the unfortunate Board of Trade was abolished in the committee by a small majority (207 to 199) of eight votes. The storm, however, blew over for a time; a large defection of country gentlemen eluded the sanguine hopes of the patriots: the Lords of Trade were revived; administration recovered their strength and spirit; and the flames of London, which were kindled by a mischievous madman, admonished all thinking men of the danger of an appeal to the people. In the premature dissolution which followed this session of parliament I lost my seat. Mr. Elliot was now deeply engaged in the measures of opposition, and the electors of Leskeard are commonly of the same opinion as Mr. Elliot.

In this interval of my senatorial life, I published the second and third volumes of the Decline and Fall. My ecclesiastical history still breathed the same spirit of freedom; but protestant zeal is more indifferent to the characters and controversies of the fourth and fifth centuries. My obstinate silence had damped the ardour of the polemics. Dr. Watson, the most candid of my adversaries, assured me that he had no thoughts of renewing the attack, and my impartial balance of the virtues and vices of Julian was generally praised. This truce was interrupted only by some animadversions of the Catholics of Italy, and by some angry letters from Mr. Travis, who made me personally responsible for condemning, with the best critics, the spurious text of the three heavenly witnesses.

The piety or prudence of my Italian translator has provided an antidote against the poison of his original. The 5th and 7th volumes are armed with five letters from an anonymous divine to his friends, Foothead and Kirk, two English students at Rome: and this meritorious service is commended by Monsignor Stoner, a prelate of the same nation, who discovers much venom in the fluid and nervous style of Gibbon. The critical essay at the end of the third volume was furnished by the Abbate Nicola Spedalieri, whose zeal has gradually swelled to a more solid confutation in two quarto volumes.—Shall I be excused for not having read them?

The brutal insolence of Mr. Travis's challenge can only be excused by the absence of learning, judgment, and humanity; and to that excuse he has the fairest or foulest pretension. Compared with Archdeacon Travis, Chelsum and Davies assume the title of respectable enemies.

The bigoted advocate of popes and monks may be turned over even to the bigots of Oxford; and the wretched Travis still smarts under the lash of the merciless Porson. I consider Mr. Porson's answer to Archdeacon Travis as the most acute and accurate piece of criticism which has appeared since the days of Bentley. His strictures are founded in argument, enriched with learning, and enlivened with wit; and his adversary neither deserves nor finds any quarter at his hands. The evidence of the three heavenly witnesses would now be rejected in any court of justice: but prejudice is blind, authority is deaf, and our vulgar bibles will ever be polluted by this spurious text, "sedet aeternumqne sedebit." The more learned ecclesiastics will indeed have the secret satisfaction of reprobating in the closet what they read in the church.

I perceived, and without surprise, the coldness and even prejudice of the town; nor could a whisper escape my ear, that, in the judgment of many readers, my continuation was much inferior to the original attempts. An author who cannot ascend will always appear to sink; envy was now prepared for my reception, and the zeal of my religious, was fortified by the motive of my political, enemies. Bishop Newton, in writing his own life, was at full liberty to declare how much he himself and two eminent brethren were disgusted by Mr. G.'s prolixity, tediousness, and affectation. But the old man should not have indulged his zeal in a false and feeble charge against the historian, who had faithfully and even cautiously rendered Dr. Burnet's meaning by the alternative of sleep or repose. That philosophic divine supposes, that, in the period between death and the resurrection, human souls exist without a body, endowed with internal consciousness, but destitute of all active or passive connection with the external world. "Secundum communem dictionem sacrae scripturae, mors dicitur somnus, et morientes dicuntur abdormire, quod innuere mihi videtur statum mortis esse statum quietis, silentii, et {Greek expression}." (De Statu Mortuorum, ch. v. p. 98.)

I was however encouraged by some domestic and foreign testimonies of applause; and the second and third volumes insensibly rose in sale and reputation to a level with the first. But the public is seldom wrong; and I am inclined to believe that, especially in the beginning, they are more prolix and less entertaining than the first: my efforts had not been relaxed by success, and I had rather deviated into the opposite fault of minute and superfluous diligence. On the Continent, my name and writings were slowly diffused; a French translation of the first volume had disappointed the booksellers of Paris; and a passage in the third was construed as a personal reflection on the reigning monarch. [Note: It may not be generally known that Louis XVI. is a great reader, and a reader of English books. On perusing a passage of my History which seems to compare him to Arcadius or Honorius, he expressed his resentment to the Prince of B—, from whom the intelligence was conveyed to me. I shall neither disclaim the allusion, nor examine the likeness; but the situation of the late King of France excludes all suspicion of flattery; and I am ready to declare that the concluding observations of my third volume were written before his accession to the throne.]

Before I could apply for a seat at the general election the list was already full; but Lord North's promise was sincere, his recommendation was effectual, and I was soon chosen on a vacancy for the borough of Lymington, in Hampshire. In the first session of the new parliament, administration stood their ground; their final overthrow was reserved for the second. The American war had once been the favourite of the country: the pride of England was irritated by the resistance of her colonies, and the executive power was driven by national clamour into the most vigorous and coercive measures. But the length of a fruitless contest, the loss of armies, the accumulation of debt and taxes, and the hostile confederacy of France, Spain, and Holland, indisposed the public to the American war, and the persons by whom it was conducted; the representatives of the people, followed, at a slow distance, the changes of their opinion; and the ministers who refused to bend, were broken by the tempest. As soon as Lord North had lost, or was about to lose, a majority in the House of Commons, he surrendered his office, and retired to a private station, with the tranquil assurance of a clear conscience and a cheerful temper: the old fabric was dissolved, and the posts of government were occupied by the victorious and veteran troops of opposition. The lords of trade were not immediately dismissed, but the board itself was abolished by Mr. Burke's bill, which decency had compelled the patriots to revive; and I was stripped of a convenient salary, after having enjoyed it about three years.

So flexible is the title of my History, that the final aera might be fixed at my own choice; and I long hesitated whether I should be content with the three volumes, the fall of the Western empire, which fulfilled my first engagement with the public. In this interval of suspense, nearly a twelvemonth, I returned by a natural impulse to the Greek authors of antiquity; I read with new pleasure the Iliad and the Odyssey, the Histories of Herodotus, Thucydides, and Xenophon, a large portion of the tragic and comic theatre of Athens, and many interesting dialogues of the Socratic school. Yet in the luxury of freedom I began to wish for the daily task, the active pursuit, which gave a value to every book, and an object to every inquiry; the preface of a new edition announced my design, and I dropped without reluctance from the age of Plato to that of Justinian. The original texts of Procopius and Agathias supplied the events and even the characters of his reign: but a laborious winter was devoted to the Codes, the Pandects, and the modern interpreters, before I presumed to form an abstract of the civil law. My skill was improved by practice, my diligence perhaps was quickened by the loss of office; and, excepting the last chapter, I had finished the fourth volume before I sought a retreat on the banks of the Leman Lake.

It is not the purpose of this narrative to expatiate on the public or secret history of the times: the schism which followed the death of the Marquis of Rockingham, the appointment of the Earl of Shelburne, the resignation of Mr. Fox, and his famous coalition with Lord North. But I may assert, with some degree of assurance, that in their political conflict those great antagonists had never felt any personal animosity to each other, that their reconciliation was easy and sincere, and that their friendship has never been clouded by the shadow of suspicion or jealousy. The most violent or venal of their respective followers embraced this fair occasion of revolt, but their alliance still commanded a majority in the House of Commons; the peace was censured, Lord Shelburne resigned, and the two friends knelt on the same cushion to take the oath of secretary of state. From a principle of gratitude I adhered to the coalition: my vote was counted in the day of battle, but I was overlooked in the division of the spoil. There were many claimants more deserving and importunate than myself: the board of trade could not be restored; and, while the list of places was curtailed, the number of candidates was doubled. An easy dismission to a secure seat at the board of customs or excise was promised on the first vacancy: but the chance was distant and doubtful; nor could I solicit with much ardour an ignoble servitude, which would have robbed me of the most valuable of my studious hours: at the same time the tumult of London, and the attendance on parliament, were grown more irksome; and, without some additional income, I could not long or prudently maintain the style of expence to which I was accustomed.

From my early acquaintance with Lausanne I had always cherished a secret wish, that the school of my youth might become the retreat of my declining age. A moderate fortune would secure the blessings of ease, leisure, and independence: the country, the people, the manners, the language, were congenial to my taste; and I might indulge the hope of passing some years in the domestic society of a friend. After travelling with several English, Mr. Deyverdun was now settled at home, in a pleasant habitation, the gift of his deceased aunt: we had long been separated, we had long been silent; yet in my first letter I exposed, with the most perfect confidence, my situation, my sentiments, and my designs. His immediate answer was a warm and joyful acceptance: the picture of our future life provoked my impatience; and the terms of arrangement were short and simple, as he possessed the property, and I undertook the expence of our common house. Before I could break my English chain, it was incumbent on me to struggle with the feelings of my heart, the indolence of my temper, and the opinion of the world, which unanimously condemned this voluntary banishment. In the disposal of my effects, the library, a sacred deposit, was alone excepted: as my post-chaise moved over Westminster-bridge I bid a long farewell to the "fumum et opes strepitumque Romae." My journey by the direct road through France was not attended with any accident, and I arrived at Lausanne nearly twenty years after my second departure. Within less than three months the coalition struck on some hidden rocks: had I remained on board, I should have perished in the general shipwreck.

Since my establishment at Lausanne, more than seven years have elapsed; and if every day has not been equally soft and serene, not a day, not a moment, has occurred in which I have repented of my choice. During my absence, a long portion of human life, many changes had happened: my elder acquaintance had left the stage; virgins were ripened into matrons, and children were grown to the age of manhood. But the same manners were transmitted from one generation to another: my friend alone was an inestimable treasure; my name was not totally forgotten, and all were ambitious to welcome the arrival of a stranger and the return of a fellow-citizen. The first winter was given to a general embrace, without any nice discrimination of persons and characters. After a more regular settlement, a more accurate survey, I discovered three solid and permanent benefits of my new situation. 1. My personal freedom had been somewhat impaired by the House of Commons and the Board of Trade; but I was now delivered from the chain of duty and dependence, from the hopes and fears of political adventure: my sober mind was no longer intoxicated by the fumes of party, and I rejoiced in my escape, as often as I read of the midnight debates which preceded the dissolution of parliament. 2. My English oeconomy had been that of a solitary bachelor, who might afford some occasional dinners. In Switzerland I enjoyed at every meal, at every hour, the free and pleasant conversation of the friend of my youth; and my daily table was always provided for the reception of one or two extraordinary guests. Our importance in society is less a positive than a relative weight: in London I was lost in the crowd; I ranked with the first families of Lausanne, and my style of prudent expence enabled me to maintain a fair balance of reciprocal civilities. 3. Instead of a small house between a street and a stable-yard, I began to occupy a spacious and convenient mansion, connected on the north side with the city, and open on the south to a beautiful and boundless horizon. A garden of four acres had been laid out by the taste of Mr. Deyverdun: from the garden a rich scenery of meadows and vineyards descends to the Leman Lake, and the prospect far beyond the Lake is crowned by the stupendous mountains of Savoy. My books and my acquaintance had been first united in London; but this happy position of my library in town and country was finally reserved for Lausanne. Possessed of every comfort in this triple alliance, I could not be tempted to change my habitation with the changes of the seasons.

My friends had been kindly apprehensive that I should not be able to exist in a Swiss town at the foot of the Alps, after having so long conversed with the first men of the first cities of the world. Such lofty connections may attract the curious, and gratify the vain; but I am too modest, or too proud, to rate my own value by that of my associates; and whatsoever may be the fame of learning or genius, experience has shown the that the cheaper qualifications of politeness and good sense are of more useful currency in the commerce of life. By many, conversation is esteemed as a theatre or a school: but, after the morning has been occupied by the labours of the library, I wish to unbend rather than to exercise my mind; and in the interval between tea and supper I am far from disdaining the innocent amusement of a game at cards. Lausanne is peopled by a numerous gentry, whose companionable idleness is seldom disturbed by the pursuits of avarice or ambition: the women, though confined to a domestic education, are endowed for the most part with more taste and knowledge than their husbands and brothers: but the decent freedom of both sexes is equally remote from the extremes of simplicity and refinement. I shall add as a misfortune rather than a merit, that the situation and beauty of the Pays de Vaud, the long habits of the English, the medical reputation of Dr. Tissot, and the fashion of viewing the mountains and Glaciers, have opened us on all sides to the incursions of foreigners. The visits of Mr. and Madame Necker, of Prince Henry of Prussia, and of Mr. Fox, may form some pleasing exceptions; but, in general, Lausanne has appeared most agreeable in my eyes, when we have been abandoned to our own society. I had frequently seen Mr. Necker, in the summer of 1784, at a country house near Lausanne, where he composed his Treatise on the Administration of the Finances. I have since, in October 1790, visited him in his present residence, the castle and barony of Copet, near Geneva. Of the merits and measures of that statesman various opinions may be entertained; but all impartial men must agree in their esteem of his integrity and patriotism.

In August 1784, Prince Henry of Prussia, in his way to Paris, passed three days at Lausanne. His military conduct has been praised by professional men; his character has been vilified by the wit and malice of a daemon (Mem. Secret de la Cour de Berlin); but I was flattered by his affability, and entertained by his conversation.

In his tour of Switzerland (Sept. 1788) Mr. Fox gave me two days of free and private society. He seemed to feel, and even to envy, the happiness of my situation; while I admired the powers of a superior man, as they are blended in his attractive character with the softness and simplicity of a child. Perhaps no human being was ever more perfectly exempt from the taint of malevolence, vanity, or falsehood.

My transmigration from London to Lausanne could not be effected without interrupting the course of my historical labours. The hurry of my departure, the joy of my arrival, the delay of my tools, suspended their progress; and a full twelvemonth was lost before I could resume the thread of regular and daily industry. A number of books most requisite and least common had been previously selected; the academical library of Lausanne, which I could use as my own, contained at least the fathers and councils; and I have derived some occasional succour from the public collections of Berne and Geneva. The fourth volume was soon terminated, by an abstract of the controversies of the Incarnation, which the learned Dr. Prideaux was apprehensive of exposing to profane eyes. It had been the original design of the learned Dean Prideaux to write the history of the ruin of the Eastern Church. In this work it would have been necessary, not only to unravel all those controversies which the Christians made about the hypostatical union, but also to unfold all the niceties and subtle notions which each sect entertained concerning it. The pious historian was apprehensive of exposing that incomprehensible mystery to the cavils and objections of unbelievers: and he durst not, "seeing the nature of this book, venture it abroad in so wanton and lewd an age" (Preface to the Life of Mahomet, p. 10).

In the fifth and sixth volumes the revolutions of the empire and the world are most rapid, various, and instructive; and the Greek or Roman historians are checked by the hostile narratives of the barbarians of the East and the West. [Note: I have followed the judicious precept of the Abbe de Mably, (Maniere d'ecrire l'Hist., p. 110,) who advises the historian not to dwell too minutely on the decay of the eastern empire; but to consider the barbarian conquerors as a more worthy subject of his narrative. "Fas est et ab hoste doceri."]

It was not till after many designs, and many trials, that I preferred, as I still prefer, the method of grouping my picture by nations; and the seeming neglect of chronological order is surely compensated by the superior merits of interest and perspicuity. The style of the first volume is, in my opinion, somewhat crude and elaborate; in the second and third it is ripened into ease, correctness, and numbers; but in the three last I may have been seduced by the facility of my pen, and the constant habit of speaking one language and writing another may have infused some mixture of Gallic idioms. Happily for my eyes, I have always closed my studies with the day, and commonly with the morning; and a long, but temperate, labour has been accomplished, without fatiguing either the mind or body; but when I computed the remainder of my time and my task, it was apparent that, according to the season of publication, the delay of a month would be productive of that of a year. I was now straining for the goal, and in the last winter many evenings were borrowed from the social pleasures of Lausanne. I could now wish that a pause, an interval, had been allowed for a serious revisal.

I have presumed to mark the moment of conception: I shall now commemorate the hour of my final deliverance. It was on the day, or rather night, of the 27th of June, 1787, between the hours of eleven and twelve, that I wrote the last lines of the last page, in a summer house in my garden. After laying down my pen, I took several turns in a berceau, or covered walk of acacias, which commands a prospect of the country, the lake, and the mountains. The air was temperate, the sky was serene, the silver orb of the moon was reflected from the waters, and all nature was silent. I will not dissemble the first emotions of joy on the recovery of my freedom, and, perhaps, the establishment of my fame. But my pride was soon humbled, and a sober melancholy was spread over my mind, by the idea that I had taken an everlasting leave of an old and agreeable companion, and that whatsoever might be the future fate of my History, the life of the historian must be short and precarious. I will add two facts, which have seldom occurred in the composition of six, or at least of five quartos. 1. My first rough manuscript, without any intermediate copy, has been sent to the press. 2. Not a sheet has been seen by any human eyes, excepting those of the author and the printer: the faults and the merits are exclusively my own.

I cannot help recollecting a much more extraordinary fact, which is affirmed of himself by Retif de la Bretorme, a voluminous and original writer of French novels. He laboured, and may still labour, in the humble office of corrector to a printing-house; but this office enabled him to transport an entire volume from his mind to the press; and his work was given to the public without ever having been written with a pen.

After a quiet residence of four years, during which I had never moved ten miles from Lausanne, it was not without some reluctance and terror, that I undertook, in a journey of two hundred leagues, to cross the mountains and the sea. Yet this formidable adventure was achieved without danger or fatigue; and at the end of a fortnight I found myself in Lord Sheffield's house and library, safe, happy, and at home. The character of my friend (Mr. Holroyd) had recommended him to a seat in parliament for Coventry, the command of a regiment of light dragoons, and an Irish peerage. The sense and spirit of his political writings have decided the public opinion on the great questions of our commercial interest with America and Ireland.

The sale of his Observations on the American States was diffusive, their effect beneficial; the Navigation Act, the palladium of Britain, was defended, and perhaps saved, by his pen; and he proves, by the weight of fact and argument, that the mother-country may survive and flourish after the loss of America. My friend has never cultivated the arts of composition; but his materials are copious and correct, and he leaves on his paper the clear impression of an active and vigorous mind. His "Observations on the Trade, Manufactures, and present State of Ireland," were intended to guide the industry, to correct the prejudices, and to assuage the passions of a country which seemed to forget that she could be free and prosperous only by a friendly connection with Great Britain. The concluding observations are written with so much ease and spirit, that they may be read by those who are the least interested in the subject.

He fell (in 1784) with the unpopular coalition; but his merit has been acknowledged at the last general election, 1790, by the honourable invitation and free choice of the city of Bristol. During the whole time of my residence in England I was entertained at Sheffield-Place and in Downing-Street by his hospitable kindness; and the most pleasant period was that which I passed in the domestic society of the family. In the larger circle of the metropolis I observed the country and the inhabitants with the knowledge, and without the prejudices, of an Englishman; but I rejoiced in the apparent increase of wealth and prosperity, which might be fairly divided between the spirit of the nation and the wisdom of the minister. All party-resentment was now lost in oblivion: since I was no man's rival, no man was my enemy. I felt the dignity of independence, and as I asked no more, I was satisfied with the general civilities of the world. The house in London which I frequented with most pleasure and assiduity was that of Lord North. After the loss of power and of sight, he was still happy in himself and his friends; and my public tribute of gratitude and esteem could no longer be suspected of any interested motive. Before my departure from England, I was present at the august spectacle of Mr. Hastings's trial in Westminster Hall. It is not my province to absolve or condemn the Governor of India; but Mr. Sheridan's eloquence demanded my applause; nor could I hear without emotion the personal compliment which he paid me in the presence of the British nation.

From this display of genius, which blazed four successive days, I shall stoop to a very mechanical circumstance. As I was waiting in the managers' box, I had the curiosity to inquire of the short-hand writer, how many words a ready and rapid orator might pronounce in an hour? From 7000 to 7500 was his answer. The medium of 7200 will afford 120 words in a minute, and two words in each second. But this computation will only apply to the English language.

As the publication of my three last volumes was the principal object, so it was the first care of my English journey. The previous arrangements with the bookseller and the printer were settled in my passage through London, and the proofs, which I returned more correct, were transmitted every post from the press to Sheffield-Place. The length of the operation, and the leisure of the country, allowed some time to review my manuscript. Several rare and useful books, the Assises de Jerusalem, Ramusius de Bello Constantinopolitano, the Greek Acts of the Synod of Florence, the Statuta Urbis Romae, &c. were procured, and introduced in their proper places the supplements which they afforded. The impression of the fourth volume had consumed three months. Our common interest required that we should move with a quicker pace; and Mr. Strahan fulfilled his engagement, which few printers could sustain, of delivering every week three thousand copies of nine sheets. The day of publication was, however, delayed, that it might coincide with the fifty-first anniversary of my own birthday; the double festival was celebrated by a cheerful literary dinner at Mr. Cadell's house; and I seemed to blush while they read an elegant compliment from Mr. Hayley, whose poetical talents had more than once been employed in the praise of his friend. Before Mr. Hayley inscribed with my name his epistles on history, I was not acquainted with that amiable man and elegant poet. He afterwards thanked me in verse for my second and third volumes; and in the summer of 1781, the Roman Eagle, (a proud title) accepted the invitation of the English Sparrow, who chirped in the groves of Eartham, near Chichester. As most of the former purchasers were naturally desirous of completing their sets, the sale of the quarto edition was quick and easy; and an octavo size was printed, to satisfy at a cheaper rate the public demand. The conclusion of my work was generally read, and variously judged. The style has been exposed to much academical criticism; a religious clamour was revived, and the reproach of indecency has been loudly echoed by the rigid censors of morals. I never could understand the clamour that has been raised against the indecency of my three last volumes. 1. An equal degree of freedom in the former part, especially in the first volume, had passed without reproach. 2. I am justified in painting the manners of the times; the vices of Theodora form an essential feature in the reign and character of Justinian. 3. My English text is chaste, and all licentious passages are left in the obscurity of a learned language. Le Latin dans ses mots brave l'honnetete, says the correct Boileau, in a country and idiom more scrupulous than our own. Yet, upon the whole, the History of the Decline and Fall seems to have struck root, both at home and abroad, and may, perhaps, a hundred years hence still continue to be abused. I am less flattered by Mr. Porson's high encomium on the style and spirit of my history, than I am satisfied with his honourable testimony to my attention, diligence, and accuracy; those humble virtues, which religious zeal had most audaciously denied. The sweetness of his praise is tempered by a reasonable mixture of acid. As the book may not be common in England, I shall transcribe my own character from the Bibliotheca Historica of Meuselius, a learned and laborious German. "Summis aevi nostri historicis Gibbonus sine dubio adnumerandus est. Inter capitolii ruinas stans primum hujus operis scribendi concilium cepit. Florentissimos vitae annos colligendo et laborando eidem impendit. Enatum inde monumentum aere perennius, licet passim appareant sinistre dicta, minus perfecta, veritati non satis consentanea. Videmus quidem ubique fere studium scrutandi veritatemque scribendi maximum: tamen sine Tillemontio duce ubi scilicet hujus historia finitur saepius noster titubat atque hallucinatur. Quod vel maxime fit ubi de rebus Ecclesiasticis vel de juris prudentia Romana (tom. iv.) tradit, et in aliis locis. Attamen naevi hujus generis haud impediunt quo minus operis summam et {Greek} praedare dispositam, delectum rerum sapientissimum, argutum quoque interdum, dictionemque seu stylum historico aeque ac philosopho dignissimum, et vix a quoque alio Anglo, Humio ac Robertsono haud exceptis (praereptum?) vehementer laudemus, atque saeculo nostro de hujusmodi historia gratulemur . . . . Gibbonus adversaries cum in tum extra patriam nactus est, quia propogationem religionis Christianae, non, tit vulgo, fieri solet, cut more Theologorum, sed ut Historicum et Philosophum decet, exposuerat."

The French, Italian, and German translations have been executed with various success; but, instead of patronizing, I should willingly suppress such imperfect copies, which injure the character, while they propagate the name of the author. The first volume had been feebly, though faithfully, translated into French by M. Le Clerc de Septchenes, a young gentleman of a studious character and liberal fortune. After his decease the work was continued by two manufacturers of Paris, M. M. Desmuniers and Cantwell: but the former is now an active member in the national assembly, and the undertaking languishes in the hands of his associate. The superior merit of the interpreter, or his language, inclines me to prefer the Italian version: but I wish that it were in my power to read the German, which is praised by the best judges. The Irish pirates are at once my friends and my enemies, But I cannot be displeased with the too numerous and correct impressions which have been published for the use of the continent at Basil in Switzerland. [Note: Of their 14 8vo. vols. the two last include the whole body of the notes. The public importunity had forced me to remove them from the end of the volume to the bottom of the page; but I have often repented of my compliance.] The conquests of our language and literature are not confined to Europe alone, and a writer who succeeds in London, is speedily read on the banks of the Delaware and the Ganges.

In the preface of the fourth volume, while I gloried in the name of an Englishman, I announced my approaching return to the neighbourhood of the Lake of Lausanne. This last trial confirmed my assurance that I had wisely chosen for my own happiness; nor did I once, in a year's visit, entertain a wish of settling in my native country. Britain is the free and fortunate island; but where is the spot in which I could unite the comforts and beauties of my establishment at Lausanne? The tumult of London astonished my eyes and ears; the amusements of public places were no longer adequate to the trouble; the clubs and assemblies were filled with new faces and young men; and our best society, our long and late dinners, would soon have been prejudicial to my health. Without any share in the political wheel, I must be idle and insignificant: yet the most splendid temptations would not have enticed me to engage a second time in the servitude of Parliament or office. At Tunbridge, some weeks after the publication of my History,

I reluctantly quitted Lord and Lady Sheffield, and, with a young Swiss friend, M. Wilhelm. de Severy, whom I had introduced to the English world, I pursued the road of Dover and Lausanne. My habitation was embellished in my absence, and the last division of books, which followed my steps, increased my chosen library to the number of between six and seven thousand volumes. My seraglio was ample, my choice was free, my appetite was keen. After a full repast on Homer and Aristophanes, I involved myself in the philosophic maze of the writings of Plato, of which the dramatic is, perhaps, more interesting than the argumentative part: but I stepped aside into every path of inquiry which reading or reflection accidentally opened.

Alas! the joy of my return, and my studious ardour, were soon damped by the melancholy state of my friend Mr. Deyverdun. His health and spirits had long suffered a gradual decline, a succession of apoplectic fits announced his dissolution; and before he expired, those who loved him could not wish for the continuance of his life. The voice of reason might congratulate his deliverance, but the feelings of nature and friendship could be subdued only by time: his amiable character was still alive in my remembrance; each room, each walk, was imprinted with our common footsteps; and I should blush at my own philosophy, if a long interval of study had not preceded and followed the death of my friend. By his last will he left to me the option of purchasing his house and garden, or of possessing them during my life, on the payment either of a stipulated price, or of an easy retribution to his kinsman and heir. I should probably have been tempted by the daemon of property, if some legal difficulties had not been started against my title; a contest would have been vexatious, doubtful, and invidious; and the heir most gratefully subscribed an agreement, which rendered my life-possession more perfect, and his future condition more advantageous. Yet I had often revolved the judicious lines in which Pope answers the objections of his longsighted friend:

> Pity to build without or child or wife;
> Why, you'll enjoy it only all your life
> Well, if the use be mine, does it concern one,
> Whether the name belong to Pope or Vernon?

The certainty of my tenure has allowed me to lay out a considerable sum in improvements and alterations: they have been executed with skill and taste; and few men of letters, perhaps, in Europe, are so desirably lodged as myself. But I feel, and with the decline of years I shall more painfully feel, that I am alone in Paradise. Among the circle of my acquaintance at Lausanne, I have gradually acquired the solid and tender friendship of a respectable family, the family of de Severy: the four persons of whom it is composed are all endowed with the virtues best adapted to their age and situation; and I am encouraged to love the parents as a brother, and the children as a father. Every day we seek and find the opportunities of meeting: yet even this valuable connection cannot supply the loss of domestic society.

Within the last two or three years our tranquillity has been clouded by the disorders of France: many families at Lausanne were alarmed and affected by the terrors of an impending bankruptcy; but the revolution, or rather the dissolution of the kingdom has been heard and felt in the adjacent lands.

I beg leave to subscribe my assent to Mr. Burke's creed on the revolution of France. I admire his eloquence, I approve his politics, I adore his chivalry, and I can almost excuse his reverence for church establishments. I have sometimes thought of writing a dialogue of the dead, in which Lucian, Erasmus, and Voltaire should mutually acknowledge the danger of exposing an old superstition to the contempt of the blind and fanatic multitude.

A swarm of emigrants of both sexes, who escaped from the public ruin, has been attracted by the vicinity, the manners, and the language of Lausanne; and our narrow habitations in town and country are now occupied by the first names and titles of the departed monarchy. These noble fugitives are entitled to our pity; they may claim our esteem, but they cannot, in their present state of mind and fortune, much contribute to our amusement. Instead of looking down as calm and idle spectators on the theatre of Europe, our domestic harmony is somewhat embittered by the infusion of party spirit: our ladies and gentlemen assume the character of self-taught politicians; and the sober dictates of wisdom and experience are silenced by the clamour of the triumphant democrates. The fanatic missionaries of sedition have scattered the seeds of discontent in our cities and villages, which had flourished above two hundred and fifty years without fearing the approach of war, or feeling the weight of government. Many individuals, and some communities, appear to be infested with the Gallic phrenzy, the wild theories of equal and boundless freedom; but I trust that the body of the people will be faithful to their sovereign and to themselves; and I am satisfied that the failure or success of a revolt would equally terminate in the ruin of the country. While the aristocracy of Berne protects the happiness, it is superfluous to enquire whether it be founded in the rights of man: the oeconomy of the state is liberally supplied without the aid of taxes; and the magistrates must reign with prudence and equity, since they are unarmed in the midst of an armed nation.

The revenue of Berne, excepting some small duties, is derived from church lands, tithes, feudal rights, and interest of money. The republic has nearly 500,000 pounds sterling in the English funds, and the amount of their treasure is unknown to the citizens themselves. For myself (may the omen be averted) I can only declare, that the first stroke of a rebel drum would be the signal of my immediate departure.

When I contemplate the common lot of mortality, I must acknowledge that I have drawn a high prize in the lottery of life. The far greater part of the globe is overspread with barbarism or slavery: in the civilized world, the most numerous class is condemned to ignorance and poverty; and the double fortune of my birth in a free and enlightened country, in an honourable and wealthy family, is the lucky chance of an unit against millions. The general probability is about three to one, that a new-born infant will not live to complete his fiftieth year. [Note: Buffon, Supplement a l'Hist. naturelle, vii. p, 158-164, of a given number of new-born infants, one half, by the fault of nature or man, is extinguished before the age of puberty and reason,—a melancholy calculation!] I have now passed that age, and may fairly estimate the present value of my existence in the three-fold division of mind, body, and estate.

1. The first and indispensable requisite of happiness is a clear conscience, unsullied by the reproach or remembrance of an unworthy action.

—Hic murus aheneus esto,
Nil conscire sibi, nulla pallescere culpa.

I am endowed with a cheerful temper, a moderate sensibility, and a natural disposition to repose rather than to activity: some mischievous appetites and habits have perhaps been corrected by philosophy or time. The love of study, a passion which derives fresh vigour from enjoyment, supplies each day, each hour, with a perpetual source of independent and rational pleasure; and I am not sensible of any decay of the mental faculties. The original soil has been highly improved by cultivation; but it may be questioned, whether some flowers of fancy, some grateful errors, have not been eradicated with the weeds of prejudice.

2. Since I have escaped from the long perils of my childhood, the serious advice of a physician has seldom been requisite. "The madness of superfluous health" I have never known; but my tender constitution has been fortified by time, and the inestimable gift of the sound and peaceful slumbers of infancy may be imputed both to the mind and body.

3. I have already described the merits of my society and situation; but these enjoyments would be tasteless or bitter if their possession were not assured by an annual and adequate supply. According to the scale of Switzerland, I am a rich man; and I am indeed rich, since my income is superior to my expence, and my expence is equal to my wishes. My friend Lord Sheffield has kindly relieved me from the cares to which my taste and temper are most adverse: shall I add, that since the failure of my first wishes, I have never entertained any serious thoughts of a matrimonial connection?

I am disgusted with the affectation of men of letters, who complain that they have renounced a substance for a shadow; and that their fame (which sometimes is no insupportable weight) affords a poor compensation for envy, censure, and persecution. [Note: M. d'Alembert relates, that as he was walking in the gardens of Sans Souci with the King of Prussia, Frederic said to him, "Do you see that old woman, a poor weeder, asleep on that sunny bank? she is probably a more happy being than either of us." The king and the philosopher may speak for themselves; for my part I do not envy the old woman.] My own experience, at least, has taught me a very different lesson: twenty happy years have been animated by the labour of my History; and its success has given me a name, a rank, a character, in the world, to which I should not otherwise have been entitled. The freedom of my writings has indeed provoked an implacable tribe; but, as I was safe from the stings, I was soon accustomed to the buzzing of the hornets: my nerves are not tremblingly alive, and my literary temper is so happily framed, that I am less sensible of pain than of pleasure. The rational pride of an author may be offended, rather than flattered, by vague indiscriminate praise; but he cannot, he should not, be indifferent to the fair testimonies of private and public esteem. Even his moral sympathy may be gratified by the idea, that now, in the present hour, he is imparting some degree of amusement or knowledge to his friends in a distant land: that one day his mind will be familiar to the grand-children of those who are yet unborn. I cannot boast of the friendship or favour of princes; the patronage of English literature has long since been devolved on our booksellers, and the measure of their liberality is the least ambiguous test of our common success. Perhaps the golden mediocrity of my fortune has contributed to fortify my application.

The present is a fleeting moment, the past is no more; and our prospect of futurity is dark and doubtful. This day may possibly be my last: but the laws of probability, so true in general, so fallacious in particular, still allow about fifteen years. [Mr. Buffon, from our disregard of the possibility of death within the four and twenty hours, concludes that a chance, which falls below or rises above ten thousand to one, will never affect the hopes or fears of a reasonable man. The fact is true, but our courage is the effect of thoughtlessness, rather than of reflection. If a public lottery were drawn for, the choice of an immediate victim, and if our name were inscribed on ore of the ten thousand tickets, should we be perfectly easy?] I shall soon enter into the period which, as the most agreeable of my long life, was selected by the judgment and experience of the sage Fontenelle. His choice is approved by the eloquent historian of nature, who fixes our moral happiness to the mature season in which our passions are supposed to be calmed, our duties fulfilled, our ambition satisfied, our fame and fortune established on a solid basis (see Buffon). In private conversation, that great and amiable man added the weight of his own experience; and this autumnal felicity might be exemplified in the lives of Voltaire, Hume, and many other men of letters. I am far more inclined to embrace than to dispute this comfortable doctrine. I will not suppose any premature decay of the mind or body; but I must reluctantly observe that two causes, the abbreviation of time, and the failure of hope, will always tinge with a browner shade the evening of life.

[POSTSCRIPT BY LORD SHEFFIELD]

WHEN I first undertook to prepare Mr. Gibbon's Memoirs for the Press, I supposed that it would be necessary to introduce some continuation of them, from the time when they cease, namely, soon after his return to Switzerland in the year 1788; but the examination of his correspondence with me suggested, that the best continuation would be the publication of his letters from that time to his death. I shall thus give more satisfaction, by employing the language of Mr. Gibbon, instead of my own; and the public will see him in a new and (I think) an admirable light, as a writer of letters. By the insertion of a few occasional sentences, I shall obviate the disadvantages that are apt to arise from an interrupted narration. A prejudiced or a fastidious critic may condemn, perhaps, some parts of the letters as trivial; but many readers, I flatter myself, will be gratified by discovering even in these my friend's affectionate feelings, and his character in familiar life. His letters in general bear a strong resemblance to the style and turn of his conversation; the characteristics of which were vivacity, elegance, and precision, with knowledge astonishingly extensive and correct. He never ceased to be instructive and entertaining; and in general there was a vein of pleasantry in his conversation which prevented its becoming languid, even during a residence of many months with a family in the country.

It has been supposed that he always arranged what he intended to say, before he spoke; his quickness in conversation contradicts this notion: but it is very true, that before he sat down to write a note or letter, he completely arranged in his mind what he meant to express. He pursued the same method in respect to other composition; and he occasionally would walk several times about his apartment before he had rounded a period to his taste. He has pleasantly remarked to me, that it sometimes cost him many a turn before he could throw a sentiment into a form that gratified his own criticism. His systematic habit of arrangement in point of style, assisted, in his instance, by an excellent memory and correct judgment, is much to be recommended to those who aspire to any perfection in writing.

Although the Memoirs extend beyond the time of Mr. Gibbon's return to Lausanne, I shall insert a few Letters, written immediately after his arrival there, and combine them so far as to include even the last note which he wrote a few days previously to his death. Some of them contain few incidents; but they connect and carry on the account either of his opinions or of his employment.

BIBLIOBAZAAR

The essential book market!

Did you know that you can get any of our titles in large print?

Did you know that we have an ever-growing collection of books in many languages?

Order online:
www.bibliobazaar.com

Find all of your favorite classic books!

Stay up to date with the latest government reports!

At BiblioBazaar, we aim to make knowledge more accessible by making thousands of titles available to you- *quickly and affordably*.

Contact us:
BiblioBazaar
PO Box 21206
Charleston, SC 29413